STRATA
a desert dwelling

STRATA
a desert dwelling

James Moore McCown

Drewett Works
David Michael Miller Associates
Desert Star Construction

foreword by C.P. Drewett
edited by Oscar Riera Ojeda
photography by Werner Segarra

OSCAR RIERA OJEDA
PUBLISHERS

14

foreword
by C.P. Drewett

18

building in the
sonoran desert
by James Moore McCown

24

architecture

110

strata:
a desert dwelling
by James Moore McCown

116

interiors

206

construction

254

photography credits

262

project credits

263

company profiles

264

contributors

268

book credits

foreword

by C.P. Drewett

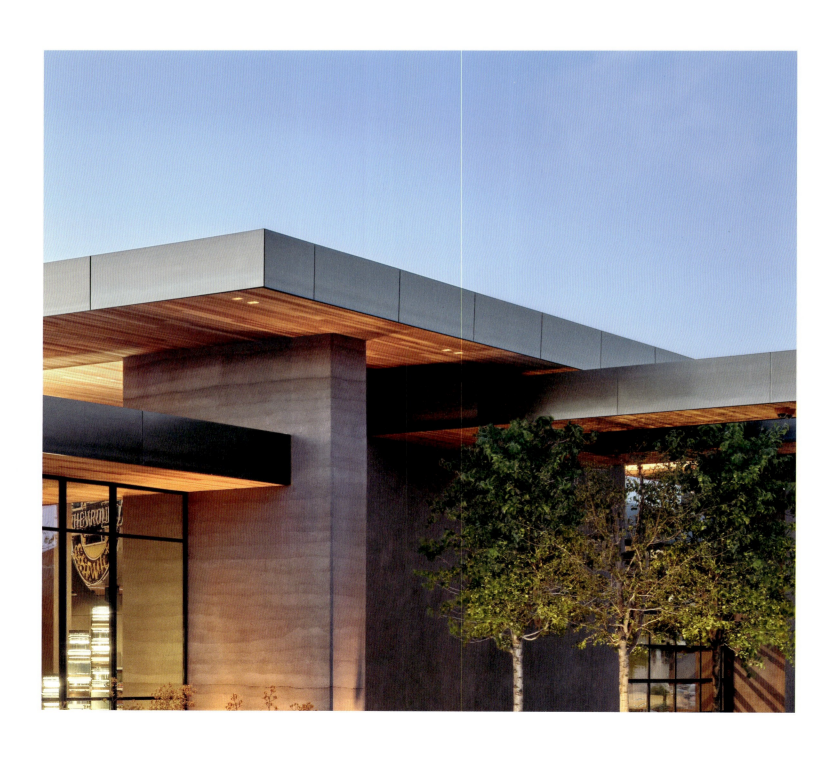

"Be not afraid of greatness. Some are born great, some achieve greatness, and others have greatness thrust upon them."
— William Shakespeare.

That moment — when you are allowed to be the best of what you are and hope to be — is daunting, to be sure. This site, this client, and knowing that this project would be historic for the region raised expectations to an intimidating height. I must explore the depths of all I know, as greatness would be required for this. I must trust that my Creator used every moment of my life, education, and experience to prepare me.

Spinning and overwhelmed, joyful and intimidated, I felt many emotions as I walked the remarkable STRATA site for the first time. Endless views and possibilities surrounded me as I surveyed the 250+ acres of the Sonoran Desert.

How would I tame infinity?

It begins with a clean drawing board, a roll of buff paper, and my favorite assortment of pens and pencils. Beneath the buff paper, a survey of the property peeks through. From this vantage point, the challenges of the site present themselves to me — elevation changes, sight lines, distant vistas, and desert washes — meandering throughout the potential building envelope. At this moment, my brain fuses science and art.

The answer? Minimalism of form. Simplicity of materials. STRATA was to be epic in its size and scope. And so, I had to distill architectural ideas down to their bare essence. The resulting materials palette contains four elements: rammed earth, glass, wood, and steel. Like the French philosopher Blaise Pascal's dictum that it takes more time and effort to write a short letter than a long one, I labored over this monumental project until I unlocked the minimalist solution I was seeking. From these four materials would emerge the design and direction of the entire project.

I often compare what I do to a marriage. Marriage is a covenant, a bond, a commitment. Architecture is a series of marriages — the architect to the client; the architect to the collaborators; the building to the site; and finally, art to science. The pages of this book will reveal the many bonds of building to site and art to science. But I must speak to the bonds between architect and client and architect and collaborators.

There is no significant architecture without visionary clients. While STRATA's owners lacked any particular academic knowledge of architecture, they reveled in the give-and-take of the design process. They were insatiably curious and supportive of my ideas. As the project evolved, I became not just their architect but a trusted advisor, someone not trying to "sell" them something but presenting ideas for the greater good of the overall project.

The bond of the architect with his collaborators was essential, a critical extension of what began on my drawing board. As if handing off a newborn child, I had to pass along my design intent to be further developed by David Michael Miller Associates and later executed by Desert Star Construction. A passage from 1 Corinthians, Chapter 13, read at my wedding, reminds me of three essential elements of a relationship: faith, hope, and love. In developing this team, these would be critical. I can attest that I had faith in the team, and they had faith in me. I hoped that my vision would be multiplied by theirs, and the history of excellence brought by David Miller and Jerry and Jeremy Meek to the project would improve that vision beyond my singular efforts. Finally, there was love. We needed to love each other through any challenges and successes that might come during the six-year journey. STRATA would not have happened without these two highly talented professionals and their teams.

There are so many people to thank and acknowledge that it could fill a book. With a heart full of gratitude, I offer a special thank you to Project Manager Melissa Wastell and Project Director Rob Banach, members of the Drewett Works team. Melissa's Revit wizardry allowed concise and immediate communication with those in the field. Every project at Drewett Works exists under the careful guidance of Rob. Thank you also to every member of the DW team who touched this project along the way.

Greatness was indeed thrust upon STRATA by the talents and exceptional efforts of every designer, collaborator, artisan, and consultant. I am deeply honored to have been a part of it.

foreword

building in the sonoran desert

by James Moore McCown

ARCHITECT C.P. DREWETT'S WORK IS DEEPLY INFORMED BY THAT OF MIES VAN DER ROHE, WHOSE BARCELONA PAVILION IS PICTURED HERE.

"Like water in the desert is wisdom to the soul," wrote Australian land surveyor Edward Counsel. Indeed "soul" has played an important role in desert architecture for centuries. From the religious rituals of the Pueblo to the churches of the Spanish missionaries, the desert always had and always will have a touch of the divine, as if the clear dry air and brilliant coloration caused people to look upward in wonder.

To build in the desert is itself an act of audacity. The ancient Puebloans knew it when they constructed their stucco-clad kivas, places for sacred rites and political meetings. The Spanish conquistadors saw in the American Southwest a landscape that recalled their native Iberia; in Arizona and New Mexico, in the name of spreading Christianity, they built exquisite, jewel-like churches, also clad in stucco and meant to convert the natives to the European faith.

But it is modernist architecture and its infinite variations that found a true home in the American desert, especially the Sonoran Desert that comprises most of Arizona. Architects like Frank Lloyd Wright and Richard Neutra reveled in this exquisite blank canvas. Arizona architect Ralph E. Parachek writes eloquently: "It is a warm dry land of strong color and deep shadow, painted mountains and broad valleys, turquoise sky and long distances. A land of sunlight – bright and shining."[1]

In 1927, Wright and his entourage first came to Arizona to build the Biltmore Hotel in Phoenix. Suddenly enamored of the desert landscape, Wright was looking for a way to escape the frigid winters of his Taliesin East in Wisconsin. What a perfect place, Wright decided, for a western version of Taliesin. But first, Wright established a desert camp called Ocotillo, about which he writes:

I presently found that the white luminous canvas overhead and canvas used instead of windows afforded such agreeable diffusion of light within, was so enjoyable and sympathetic to the desert, that I now felt more oppressed by the thought of the opaque solid overhead of the much-too-heavy Midwestern house.[2]

The stock market crash of 1929 dealt a temporary blow to Wright's dream of a Taliesin West. But by the winter of 1937-1938, Wright was designing and building the desert complex, which would be his western headquarters. True to form, Wright's conception of Taliesin West was rooted in the primacy of nature. He decided to work with native stone, designing an ingenious system whereby stone was mixed with concrete. Bruce Brooks Pfeiffer explains:

Since most of the available stones had a smooth, flat face on one side, the solution presented itself thus: place the smooth surface into a temporary wooden form, the curved, boulder-like part of the stone remaining in the center of the wall like "fill." Pour concrete around the stone, moving up the surface of the wall inside the form with more stones, and more rubble-fill as required. Once set, in a day or so in this dry atmosphere, the form could be stripped, taken apart, and the lumber used over and over again to continue the wall or walls as desired.[3]

The result was like a rainbow of colors in the native stone. Contrasting are wooden elements in Wright's signature Cherokee red. In plan, the compound read as a triangle to the south and a rectangle to the northeast. A saguaro, or giant cactus, was commented on by Wright as follows: "This one, when we came here, was about half as tall as it is now, I would judge. It was quite an insignificant thing. Look at it now. It has had a family, too."[4]

Wright goes on to muse: "A characteristic thing in the desert is, of course, the desert itself. And I have always regarded it as the greatest lesson in construction. Form following function if you like – or form and function being one – that exists. The saguaro is the greatest example of a skyscraper that was ever built. I don't think we have ever built one similarly – on the same principle. We could."[5]

In contrast to Wright, the consummate American, Neutra was a European trained in the classic modernist precepts of the Bauhaus and the Wiener Werkstätte, the latter out of his native Vienna. In fact, Neutra's work in Arizona is limited. Most of his work is in California, chiefly in Palm Springs, which he and other architects turned into an "architectural playground." It is this decidedly modernist bent in which Neutra designed.

In the early 1950s, Neutra was an early proponent of what today we call "green design." He lamented that beautiful modernist works of architecture were being increasingly marginalized by worldly events. For Neutra, as described by Sylvia Lavin, "The clean space of modern abstraction was increasingly being polluted by technology and overpopulation." He and his contemporary Wilhelm Reich developed a concept of "orgone" energy, defined by Wikipedia as "a pseudoscientific concept variously described as an esoteric energy or hypothetical universal life force."[6] Lavin explains:

building in the sonoran desert

As part of continuing experiments on the healthful and restorative effects of orgone energy, [Neutra] traveled to Arizona with his cloudbusters in an effort to produce rain and purify the atmosphere. While attempting to heal the environment, Reich drew parallels between the arid terrain of the desert and what he called "the emotional desert of modern life."

Neutra too, was in the western desert in the 1950s, where he had several houses under construction.[7]

Neutra's signature desert house has many interesting elements. Chief among these was the "spider leg" column that reaches out beyond the house to form a right angle to the ground. Another was an elegant use of glass and a distinct

RICHARD NEUTRA'S DESERT HOUSE, PALM SPRINGS,.

blurring between inside and out. His use of glass, especially, stands out, as Lavin writes:

... Neutra's influential redesign of the window demonstrates that the environment reshaped postwar buildings. High modernism, in fact, had, since the early years of the century, fantasized about the transformative power of glass structures, but for the most part, the goal of architects had been to produce clarity and purity.[8]

Neutra had great faith in technology; in fact, he averred that life in the desert would be impossible without climate control:

The theory for the modern house in the desert is the same as that elsewhere – necessity. Advances in technology permit the resident of the desert to enjoy the sunshine and scenic wonders under controlled temperatures. New methods of construction and design, new systems of insulation and the use of new fabricated materials provide that desired control.[9]

Neutra was a man of deep thought and reflection, and he spelled out his theories of architecture and the human condition in a series of essays called Nature Near, published in the late 1980s, well after his death. In his introduction to this book, writer and critic William Marlin reflects on the architect's worldview:

A pragmatic idealist, weaned as much on William James and John Dewey as on William Wundt and Sigmund Freud, Neutra explored the physiological and psychological nuances of the human environment to elicit the structural, spatial and sensory character of his work. In this perspective, we can better understand why his aesthetic musings invariably reflected profound ethical and ecological sensibilities. In effect, he elevated aesthetics into the realm of euthenics ... Neutra defined biorealism as "the most practical sort of realism, taking in everything that is the body and soul of man – along with that space we call psyche, which performs as a dynamic mediator between them." Indeed, it was this inner space—this fluid, palpable sentience of man, grounded in inexorable, evolutionary rhythms – that Neutra, much as Wright before him, sought to materialize and choreograph to mellifluous practical effect.[10]

"Like water in the desert is wisdom to the soul," wrote Australian land surveyor Edward Counsel. Indeed, "soul" has played an important role in desert architecture for centuries. From the religious rituals of the Pueblo to the churches of the Spanish missionaries, the desert always had and always will have a touch of the divine, as if the clear, dry air and brilliant coloration caused people to look upward in wonder.

The Southwest continues to attract retirees and others who just want to enjoy the hot, dry air of the days and crisp, comfortable nights. But more than that, to live in Arizona is to see the crossroads of various civilizations and their ingenious adaptation to the extremes of desert life. Parachek explains: "No. The Arizona desert is no place for the hard boxwalls of the houses of the Middle West or the East. Here all is sculptured by wind and water, patterned in color and texture. Rocks and reptiles no less so than the cacti."

This book chronicles a single house that draws inspiration from the varied architectural histories and traditions of its location, as described above. Like any building in the desert, it is an act of audacity and persistence. It evinces the power of collaboration among an architect, interior designer, and construction company. STRATA: a desert dwelling is the fruit of this joint effort.

Notes:
[1] Parachek, Ralph E., *Desert Architecture*, Parr of Arizona, 1967.
[2] Futugawa, Yukio, Ed., *Frank Lloyd Wright Taliesin West*, ADA Edita Tokyo, 2002.
[3] Pfeiffer, Bruce Brooks *Frank Lloyd Wright Taliesin West*, ADA Edita Tokyo, 2002.
[4] Futagawa Ed.
[5] Ibid.
[6] Lavin, Sylvia, *Form Follows Libido: Architecture and Richard Neutra in Psychoanalytic Culture*, The MIT Press, 2004.
[7] Ibid.
[8] Ibid.
[9] Ibid.
[10] Marlin, William Ed., *Nature Near: The Late Essays of Richard Neutra*, Capra Press, 1989.
[11] Parachek.

architecture

"God is in the details." This famous aphorism is credited to the German master architect Ludwig Mies van der Rohe. It may well be apocryphal, but nonetheless, the quote has been associated with his incredible legacy since his death in 1969. This notion, and Mies's wider body of work, have greatly impacted architect C.P. Drewett in his own career. This is perhaps most apparent with STRATA.

STRATA begins with a site-driven vision. A network of rammed earth monoliths will recall indigenous architecture crafted from local soils as if they already existed on site. Stitched together by glass, these massive walls will frame a specific volumetric sequence, constrained by three different ceiling heights or horizontal datum lines. The use of these datum lines will vary based on spatial hierarchies of program adjacencies and circulation. The maze of rammed earth is then given visual clarity through these tightly defined roof planes. These broad strokes will inform the finer development of the design.

The design, at its core, is essentialist—a language distilled to its most critical components. This process of purification was unyielding, requiring extensively front-loaded detail. While schematic design sketches are classically messy with experimentation and errant line work, this "measure twice, cut once" approach rendered uncharacteristically precise hand drawings, from which a precise rule-set emerges.

A rigorous system of nested modules carefully defines material engagements. Adjacent rammed earth masses are joined by channel set glazing, allowing these liminal spaces to read as void. At the building envelope, the length of the limestone tablets—which comprise the exterior hardscape—is used to house threshold components of door jambs and air handling before continuing to the interior to frame a field of dust-on-white concrete. Next, the four-inch wide tongue-and-groove planks lay out a grid for the ceiling, demanding that all ceiling penetrations be either four or eight inches wide to preserve their cadence. This grid moves beyond the ceiling planes to define all dimensions between walls in the home. Finally, an exacting three-eighths inch reveal is maintained where any horizontal component meets a vertical component, a tolerance expertly maintained through the construction process. As a result, no walls or ceilings touch, providing space for specific surface treatments with the interior design.

While these modules operate at different scales, they interlock perfectly to form an exacting decision-making matrix.

From their broadest gestural notions to their finest details, these rules of engagement lent STRATA its voice. While this voice demanded compliance from all building components, it imbued a profound collaborative spirit into the design team, as all involved sought to harmonize within their respective disciplines. From the construction of the rammed earth formwork to the alignment of speakers…everything mattered.

Drewett gives a few closing thoughts: *It was about collaborating with others who are obsessive about getting things right – I can't tell you the number of times something was hung or attached or laid down when the team collective said, "Nope, let's do it again." Iron sharpens iron. Everyone in this project made me better. I feel that is the kinship that we share having created this together. We were all sharpened. We were all better. And we were all grateful.*

Perhaps God really is in the details.

architecture

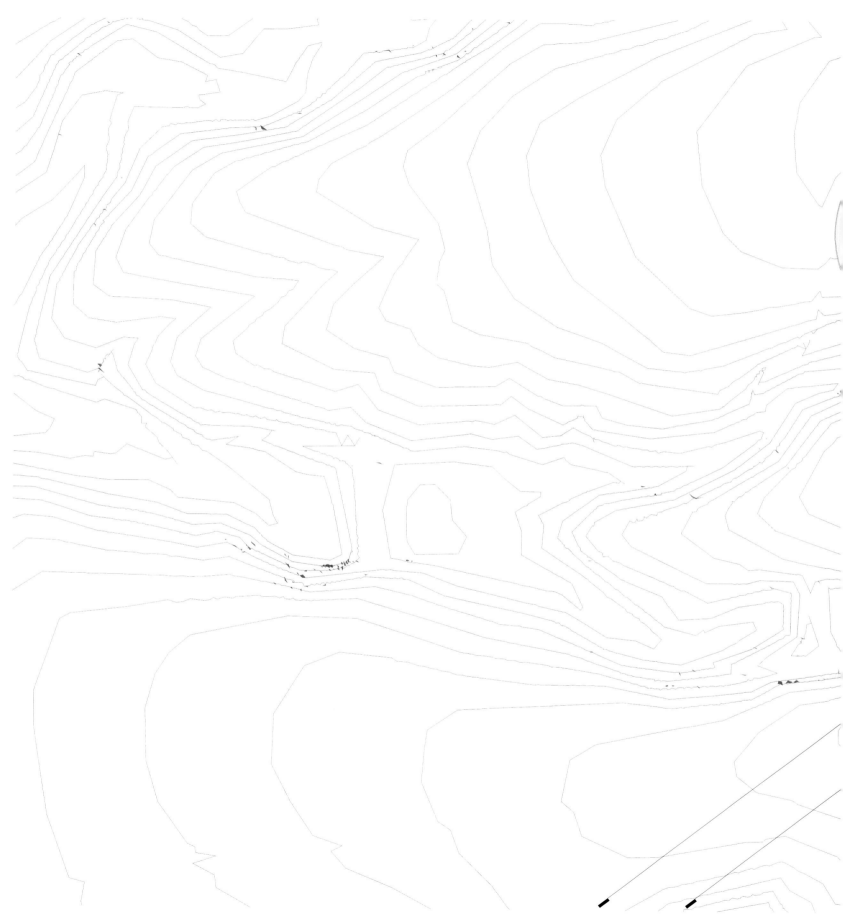

SITE PLAN

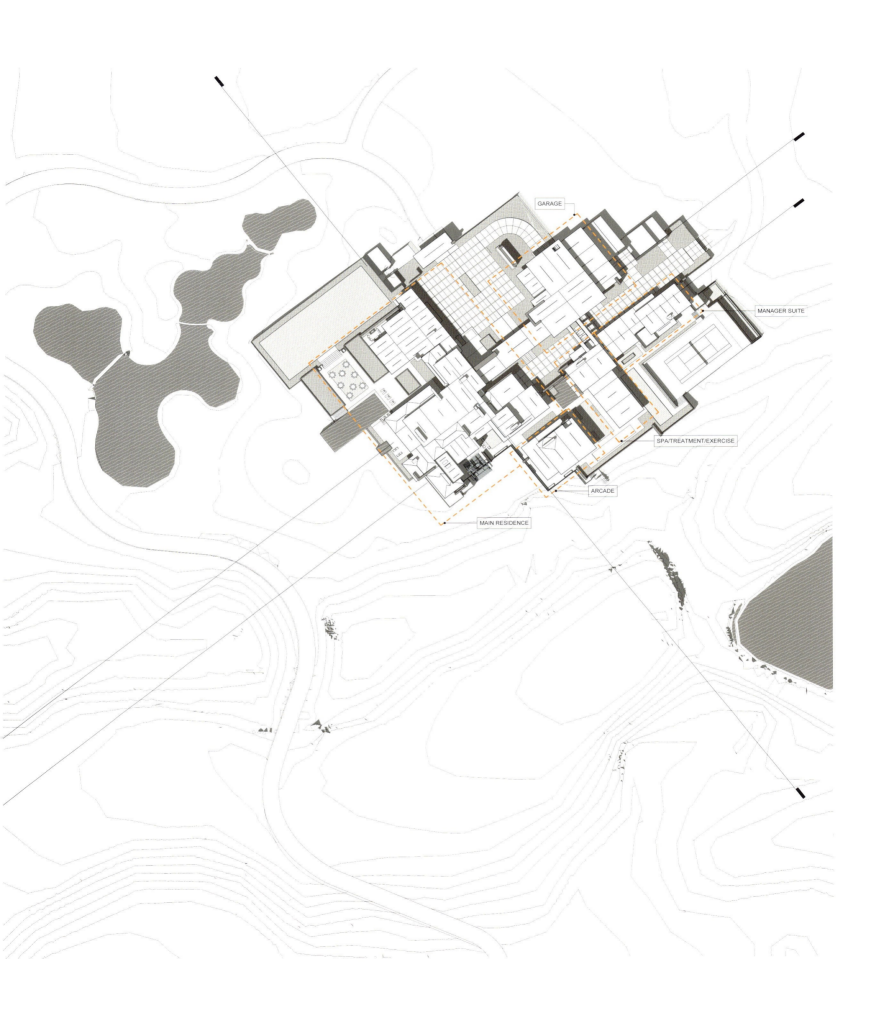

architecture

OVERALL FLOOR PLAN

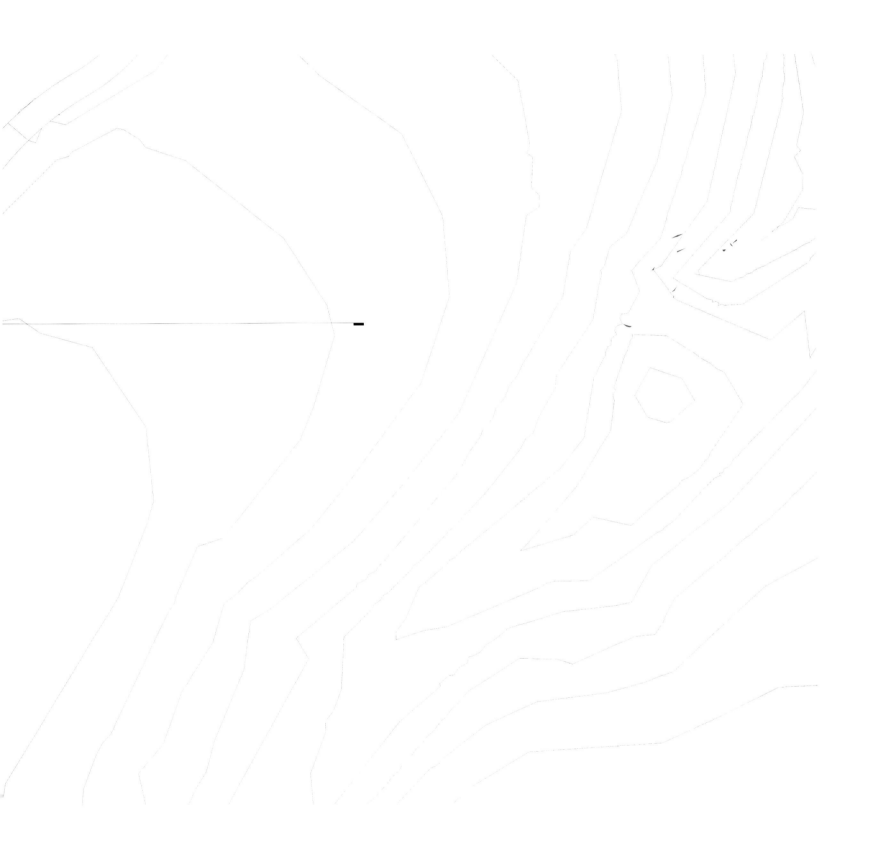

architecture

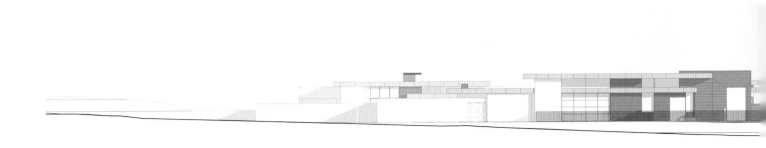

NORTH ELEVATION

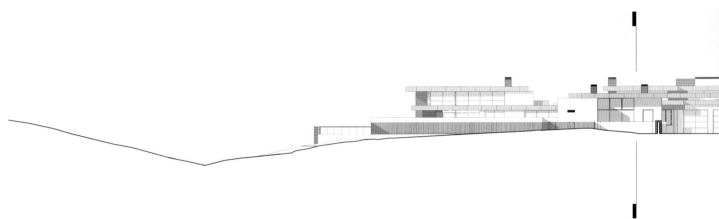

EAST ELEVATION

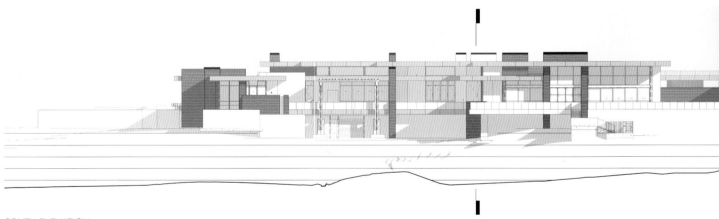

SOUTH ELEVATION

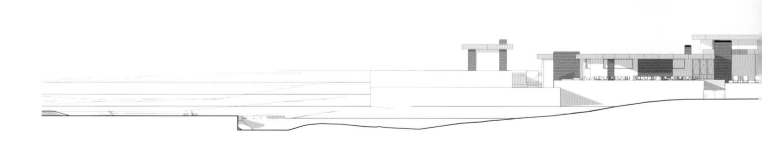

WEST ELEVATION

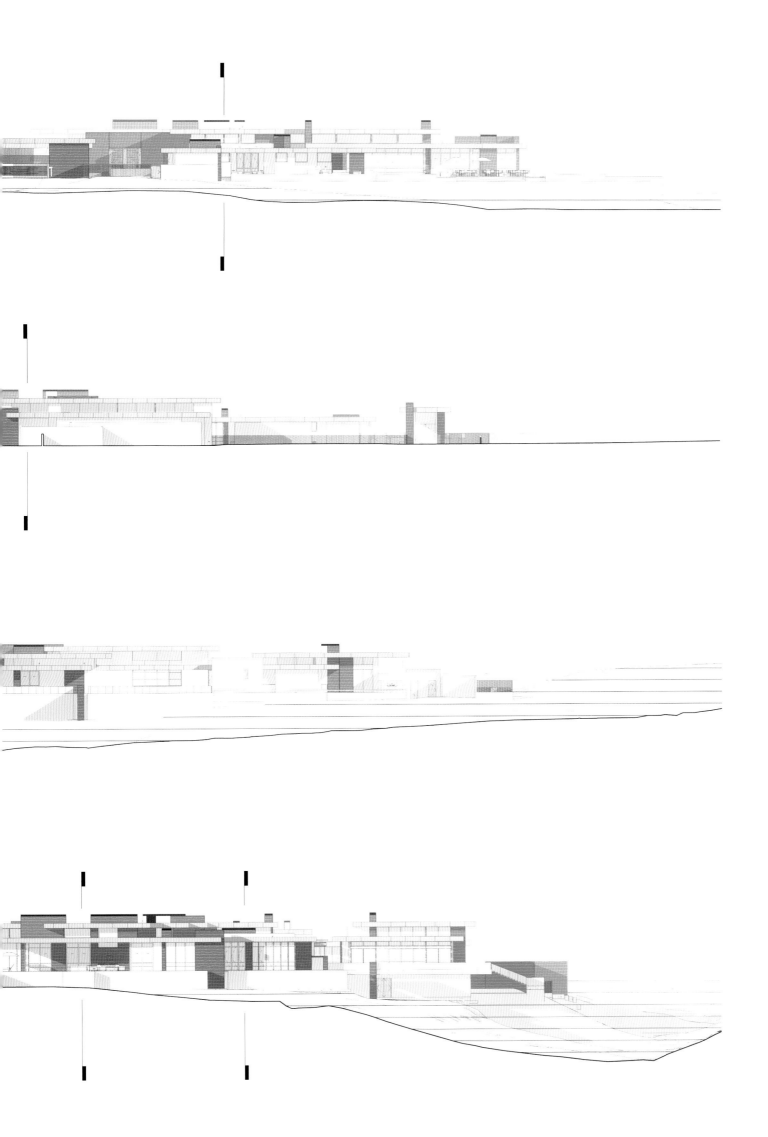

architecture

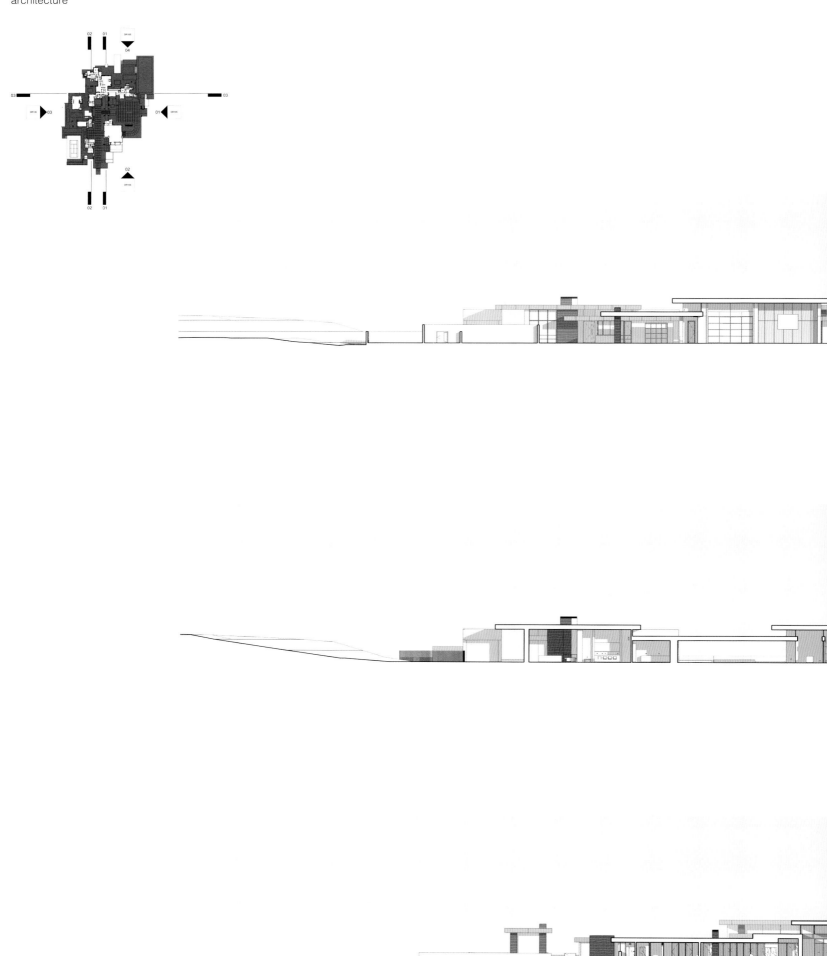

SECTIONS

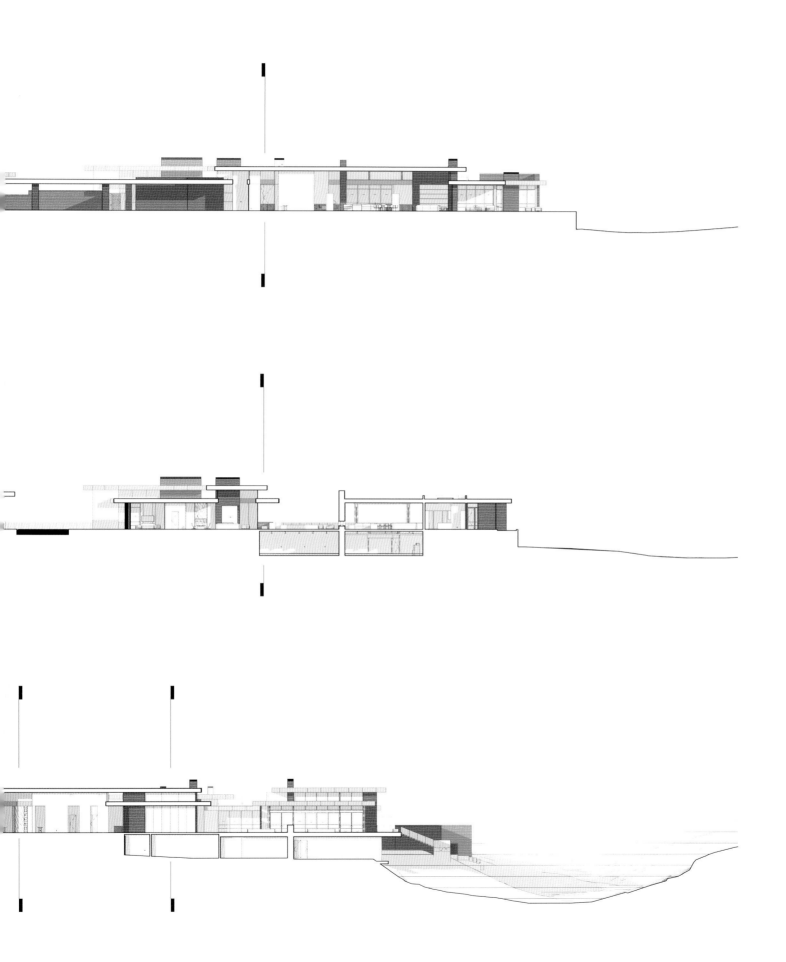

architecture

architecture

"'Less is more.'
The Miesian axiom is
perhaps most evident in
the restrained materials
palette, comprised mainly
of steel, wood, concrete,
and rammed earth."

architecture

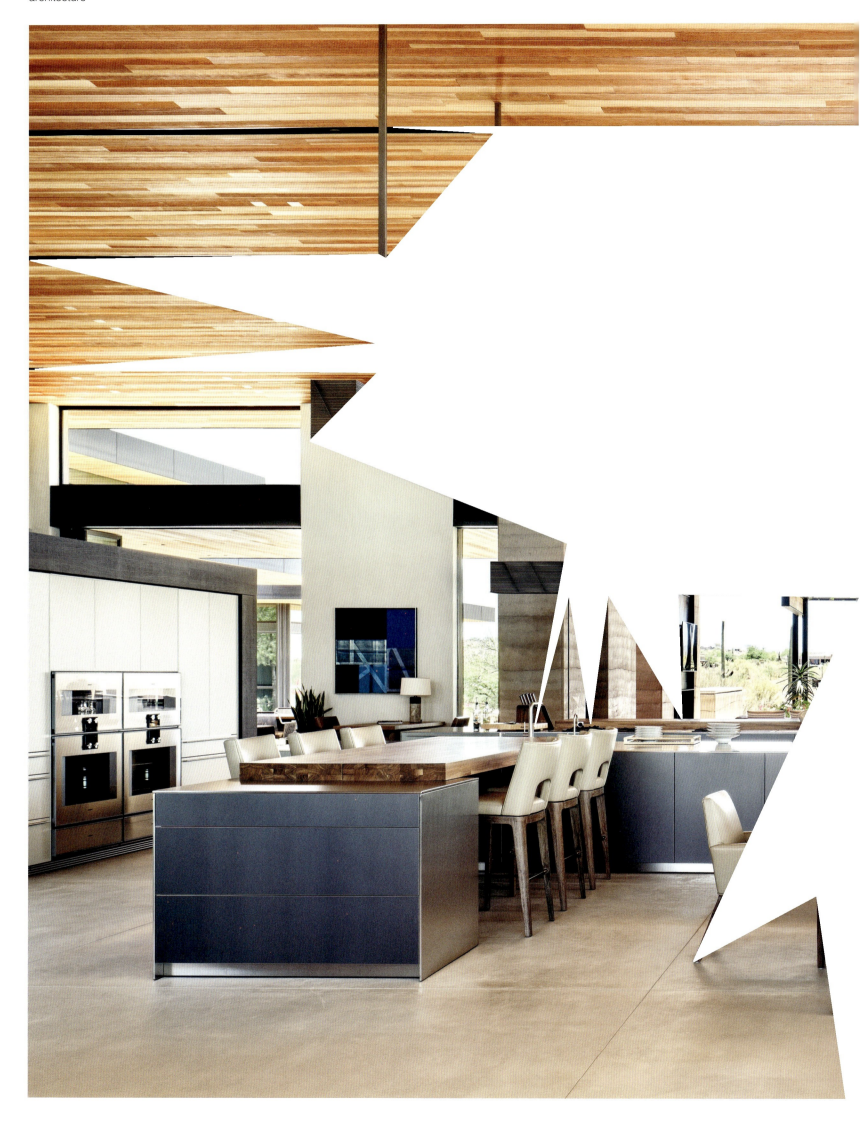

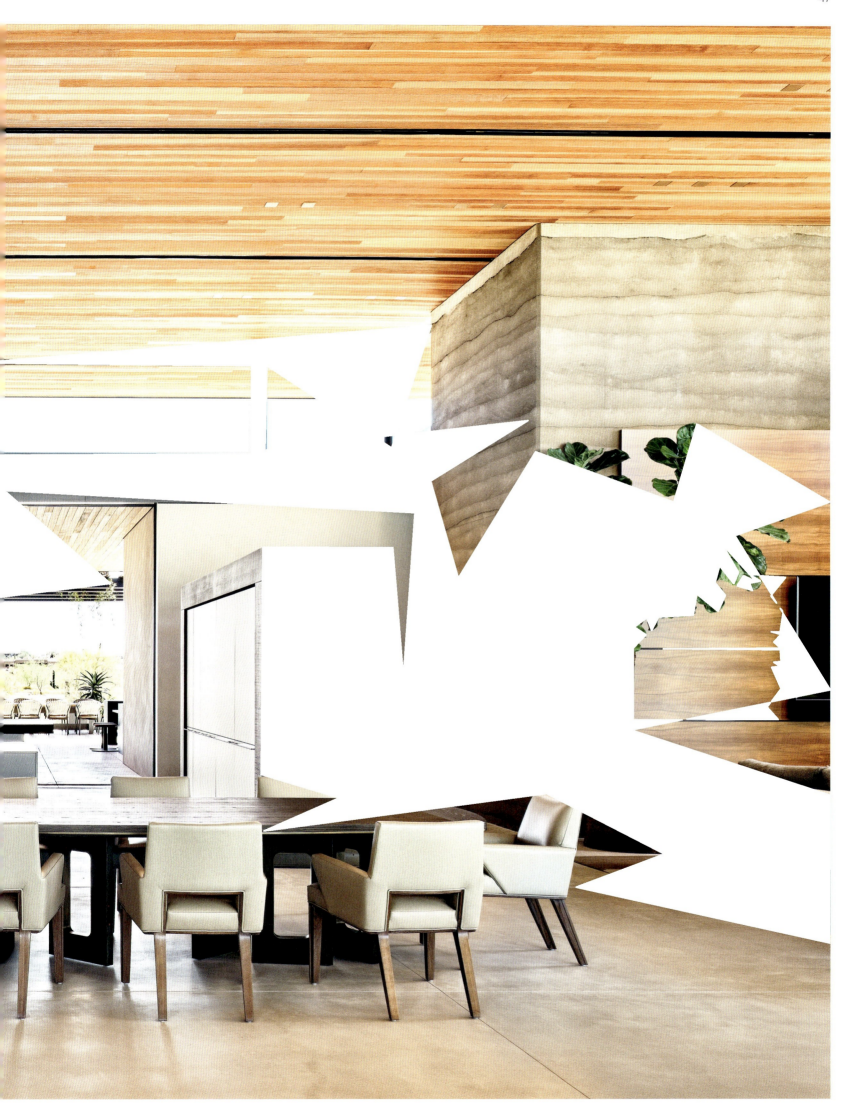

architecture

The unconventional kitchen considers cooking as a spectating event, designed in collaboration with Bulthaup.

architecture

architecture

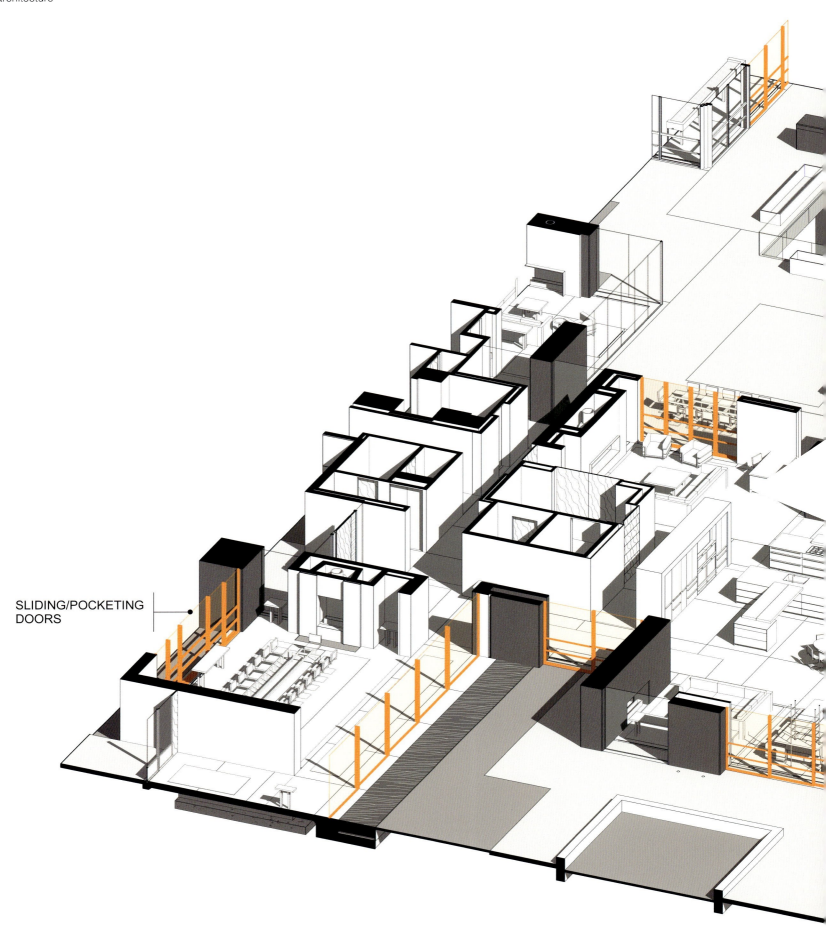

SLIDING/POCKETING DOORS

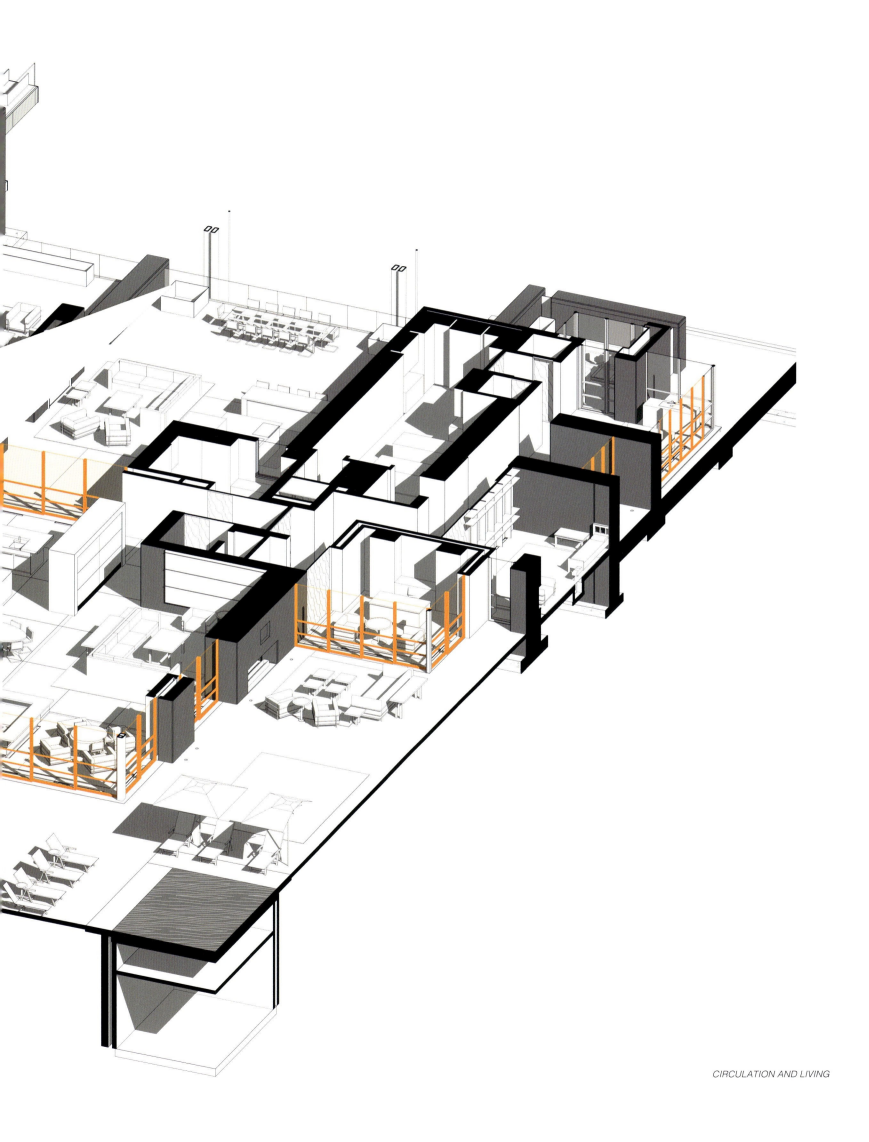

CIRCULATION AND LIVING

architecture

architecture

The clerestory glazing was designed to be as discreet as possible to express the roof planes as floating. This maximizes light penetration into the primary living spaces below.

architecture

architecture

A bold cantilever at the guest suite shades a patio. The combination of steel fascia and Douglas fir ceilings contrasts with the exterior landscaping; the entire house blurs the distinction between inside and outside.

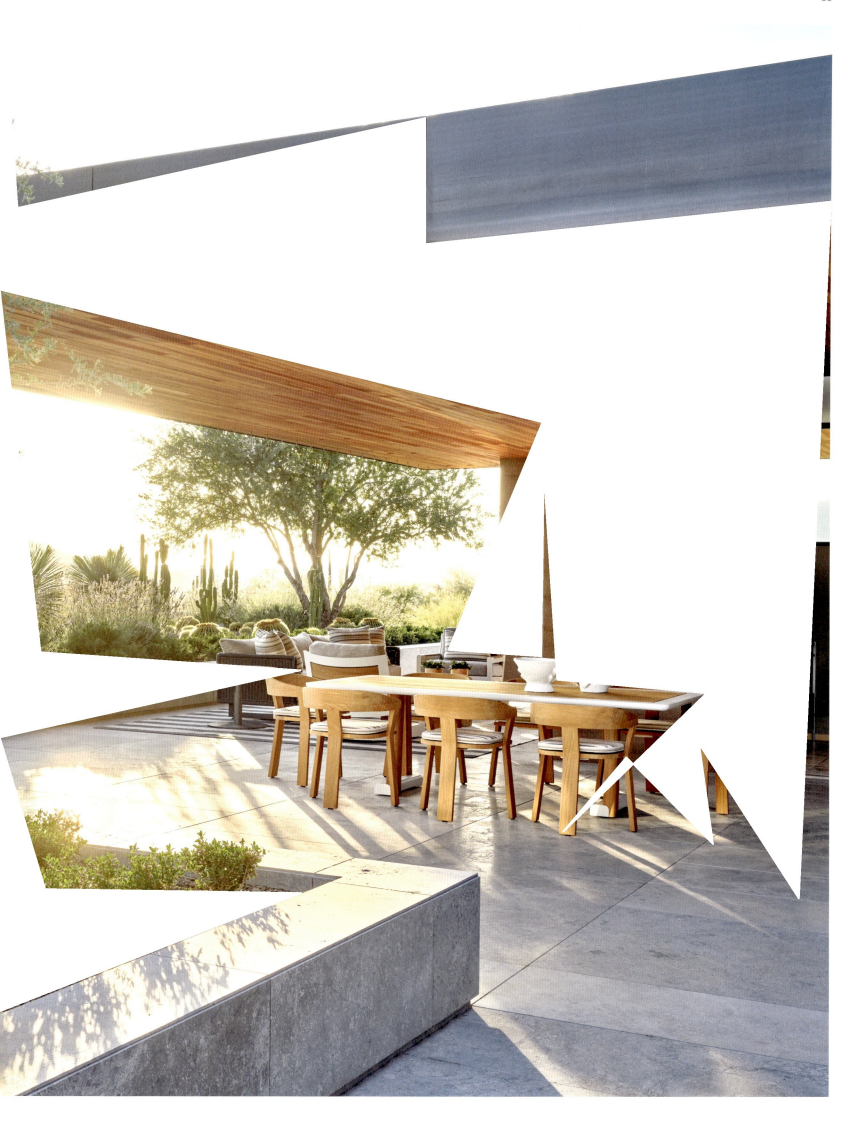

architecture

Materials meet: an integration of steel, wood, glass and rammed earth is evident in a detail of the great room fireplace. A clerestory window floods the assemblage with light.

architecture

architecture

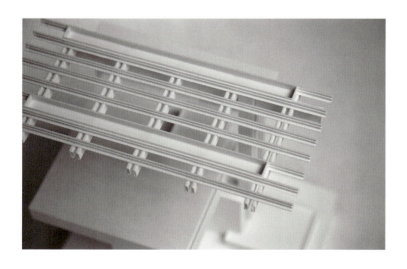

The dining trellis is a counterbalance, both in its structural composition and its relationship to the home. Nowhere else are structural elements so expressive. Draped in trailing greenery, it offers a wholly different dining experience.

architecture

These models depict segments of rammed earth and their joinery with other architectural components. The material sets the tone for the project's collaboration — a study in exacting precision and planning.

architecture

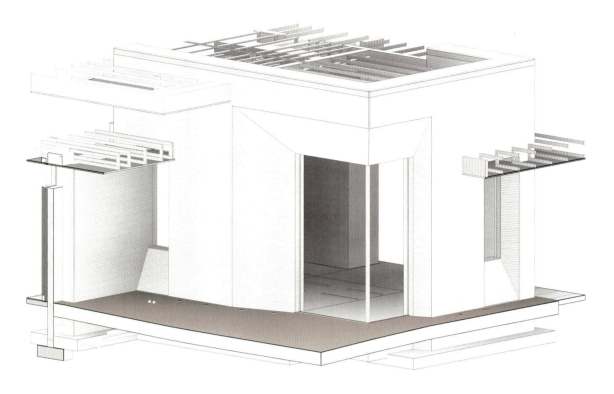

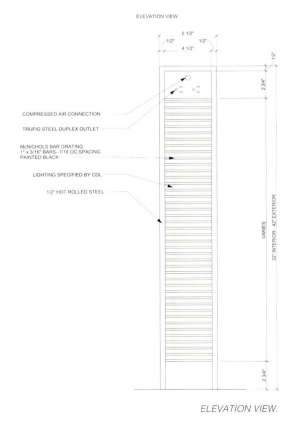

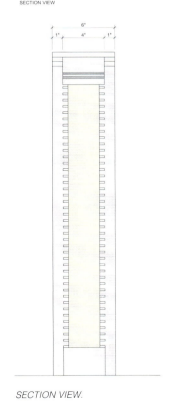

ELEVATION VIEW.   *SECTION VIEW.*

architecture

architecture

Situated at the edge of a natural wash, the residence appears to levitate, mediating between earth and sky. The color of the rich, earthen walls varies in the sunlight.

architecture

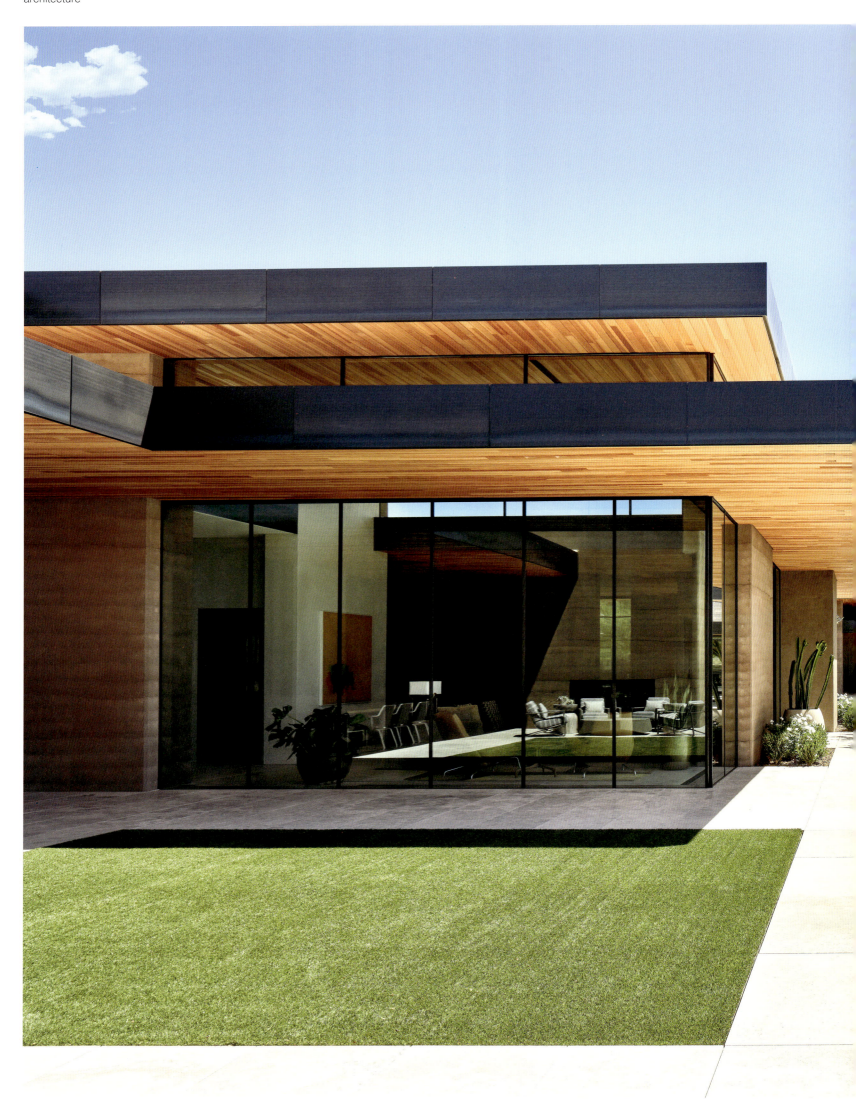

architecture

The roof heights are determined by a strict logic, varying between three horizontal datum lines based on the program underneath. This provides levity and abundant natural light.

strata:
a desert dwelling

by James Moore McCown

In her book about the work of painter Dorothea Tanning[1], British curator and art historian Catriona McAra describes the Arizona Sonoran Desert landscape that was Tanning's muse: *One can make out a pinkish tinge towards the horizon as if the convergence between land and sky had been smudged experimentally by an artist's chalk ... trifle-like layers of stratigraphy that create a gradational visual tension between the horizontal and the vertical ...*

The operant word here is "stratigraphy," defined by Webster's as "Geology that deals with the origin, composition, distribution, and succession of strata." In other words, layering, the process by which something is put one on top of the other, either naturally or by the human hand. But as equally important, layering is about how diverse architectural elements are joined in an eloquent unison; and how the multivariant collaboration essential to the craft of design and building takes place.

This book is titled *STRATA: a desert dwelling* for these very reasons. A 70,000-square-foot villa and private estate on 250+ acres in the Arizona desert is the result of a deep collaboration among an architect, an interior designer, and a construction company. It is difficult to say where the craft of Drewett Works ended and David Michael Miller Associates and Desert Star Construction picked up, so seamless and shared was the effort.

STRATA: a desert dwelling chronicles how this incredible residence, located in suburban Phoenix, was conceived and took shape; how it celebrates both indigenous building materials and the latest thinking in the accouterments of residential design; how it is beholden to some of the grandees of modernist architecture while being fresh and unique unto itself.

The sheer scale of the project is epic. The required multiple submissions of plans were each as thick as an old Manhattan telephone book; at any given time there were more than 130 construction workers on the site; and the bespoke nature of all of the elements and materials made it a logistical tour de force – even at a time of an international supply chain breakdown. It was a three-year project that wrapped just in time for COVID-19 to be announced as a global pandemic – it undoubtedly could not have so quickly been realized during the height of the worldwide outbreak.

The clients are a widely-traveled couple who own multiple other homes but consider this their primary residence. Having made their fortune in a diversified manner, the husband-and-wife team take great pleasure in hosting fundraisers for various philanthropic causes close to their hearts. They also enjoy entertaining friends and family and wanted an abode big enough to do anything they wanted.

The house sprawls around a central core. It contains multiple separate buildings, including the Main Residence, an Arcade Building for gaming and entertainment, a Wellness Pavilion, a Manager Suite for employees and a large Garage for the husband's prized collection of automobiles, new and old.

One approaches the hilly venue by meandering along a curved road, which affords sneak peeks at the house one minute then obscuring it the next, making it a true arrival sequence with a touch of architectural drama. It is akin to approaching Le Corbusier's chapel at Ronchamp, as described by Danièle Pauly:

Starting from the village of Ronchamp, the visitor takes a small steep path: having arrived at the summit of the hill, he mounts another path shaded by trees and hedges; suddenly the chapel emerges from the foliage. The initial approach to the chapel never ceases to amaze; the edifice appears one and the same time monumental and small, imposing and reassuring, disconcerting and familiar.[2]

This sense of arrival is rewarded at STRATA by the building's elegant and varied massing.

Ludwig Mies van der Rohe never designed anything in the desert Southwest, but his imprint is all over this structure. A series of orthogonal pavilions is punctuated by widely overhanging eaves, the brown tone of the earthen walls, sharply defined and elegant black steel door-and-window elements which open to the cool winter air, and mid-century furniture is visible from the outside through expansive planes of glass. As large as the house is, it is broken down into more livable, individual units, as architect C.P. Drewett explains:

This was the clients' first experience building a house. The reality of the spaces they wanted or didn't want was something that kind of grew organically. We talked about different scenarios and events and different occasions just to get to know how they would live in it and use it. But because the house is so large, there was a very deliberate attempt at creating a few destinations that live smaller. There's a two-car garage that's attached to the main house, separate from the main garage. Close to that is a smaller kitchen which we call the back kitchen and pantry. And then adjacent to that is a smaller living space that's more warm and cozy and not far from the primary suite. There's this segment of a house that lives more contained and the spaces are smaller and much more composed.

One building element that weds the house to its southwestern roots is the use of Structural Insulated Rammed Earth Walls (SIREWALL), a refined version of the earthen structures that have been a staple in the region for centuries. Jeremy Meek of Desert Star Construction describes:

The first step of constructing the rammed earth walls is assembling and setting in place the formwork: built from joists and especially smooth plywood, bound together with aluminum capture channels, and held in place with sturdy battens and anchored shoring. Thereafter, the specialty rammed earth mix will exit the on-site batch plant (volumetric mixer), be placed on a Telebelt (a conveyer for concrete) and delivered inside the forms in varied layers of color, for pneumatic ramming of the striations to occur. The rammed earth we use has a similar composition to concrete, though the biggest difference is that it's super dry – the mix has only one-half of a percent of water. More typical concrete mixes range from 30% to 60% of water content. Because there is so little water in the rammed earth mix, the setting and consolidation of the mix come through the pneumatic ramming process.

The resulting rammed earth walls are a pinnacle of beauty and practicality. They are layered one upon the other and feature a rich earthen color that changes with the region's varying sunlight. Their bands further the designers' desire to emphasize the horizontal.

"I think rammed earth lends itself to the desert and our setting and just the layers of mountains and colorization," says David Michael Miller, the interior designer. Miller knows layers and colorization well – he and his team selected the furnishings and fittings for the interior, but also designed all of the millwork and fireplaces in the home. He marshalled a rich mix of woods, metals and leather to make the interiors relatable to the architecture of the house, and also create interiors that are warming and welcoming:

We were trying to ride a stylistic line between a contemporary and modern interior. I wanted there to be texture, I wanted there to be more richness and luxury, because these inhabit the building itself so comfortably. Our selection of interior finishes and designed millwork embraces the furnishings and the way the rooms are filled. We wanted to bring intimacy and softness to all the rooms of the home. So that's why the wool fabric and the leather and the Tibetan rug used are intended to make a welcoming and inhabitable place, not just a piece of architecture. Even though the home is very large, it is still "home" for the clients, and we wanted each space to feel that way.

Architect Drewett himself was aware of the scale of the project and the need for some modesty:

Some architects rely on metaphors, some draw upon other fonts of inspiration. I'm more of an instinctive designer. Because of how overwhelming the site was, I wanted to try to solve the problem with the least amount of everything. I really wanted to compress the materials palette; I wanted things to be simple. So in my mind the house was made of four materials: the SIREWALL; the Douglas fir ceilings and under the eaves; the steel fascia on the cornices and the concrete floors. That's the palette.

According to Drewett, the elements that give the house its Miesian flair are the custom-made windows and doors, which are record-breaking in their size and weight. The largest is a 55-foot-long teak pocket door that weighs 7,200 pounds and is motorized. It opens and closes with silky precision, like the door of a new Mercedes-Benz. It blurs the inside and outside during the region's temperate autumns, winters and springs.

"There's something about Mies that informs my thoughts," Drewett says. "It's either a mass or a void. It's a wall or it's not. In this house, there's operable glass that moves and then

strata: a desert dwelling

there's glass that doesn't move and is largely channel set. It is embedded, and you see no frames."

The clients are not art collectors per se but relied on a collaboration with interior designer Miller to furnish the house with an eclectic array of works. This required several buying trips to New York, Los Angeles, and elsewhere. A color field painting by Paul Williams adds a jaunty flash to the entry foyer. In the family room, Tibetan-style rugs by Christopher Farr contrast with a painting by Paul Arnoldi. For the main dining room, a large wall-collage art piece by Doug & Mike Starn is commensurate with the size of the room. This piece, from the Lisa Sette Gallery in Phoenix, is 120" wide x 80" high.

The furniture has a modernist spirit without being rote replications of 20th-century classics. In the Conference Room for example, another Tibetan rug is matched with leather chairs by Vitra, which recall Charles and Ray Eames' and Eero Saarinen's work while having a personality of their own. Even a bathtub is turned into an objet d'art: Carved out of a single piece of stone, its sculptural form recalls a Jean Arp bird in flight.

Desert Star Construction's Meek explains how COVID-19 had the potential to sideline the entire project: "We are all very grateful we got in under the wire. February and March 2020 is when everything was shut down. Even so, a lot of people involved with the project said, 'I'll just keep on going.' We had to follow proper safety protocols that definitely bogged things down a little bit, but we were able to complete the project strongly."

Turning again to Webster's, we see the word "palimpsest" as "a writing tablet used after earlier writing has been erased," and "something having diverse layers apparent beneath the surface." So it is with STRATA: a desert dwelling. It took millions of years for nature to form the perfect desert oasis, and this canvas was an architect's, interior designer's and construction company's dream assignment. It took only five years to layer over it and transform the site into what it is today – layer upon layer upon layer.

The building does not try to replicate nature – a fool's errand under any circumstance. One of the great epiphanies of the modernist movement was its relationship to nature. For glass and steel and concrete do not in any way resemble natural forms; instead, they make nature all the more glorious in contrast.

"It is the long history of humankind ... that those who learned to collaborate and improvise most effectively have prevailed," wrote Charles Darwin.

Architect. Interior Designer. Builder. This is the triumvirate without which this project could not have been realized.

The desert does not yield itself easily. So intense co-working is necessary for any building at all, let alone one of the scope and size described herein. But the results make it worth the effort. The project has a decidedly other-worldly aura about it. British author Terry Pratchett: "Night poured over the desert. It came suddenly, in purple. In the clear air, the stars drilled down out of the sky, reminding any thoughtful watcher that it is in the deserts and high places that faiths are generated."[4]

This sacred silence has entranced the Pueblo people for uncounted millennia. Indeed as architectural historian Vincent Scully puts it: "The Great American Desert ... a place of vast silence, the pilgrimage center of the continent ... Out of those depths, the Pueblos believe their primal ancestor emerged and climbed to the upper world."[3] Scully continues to marvel at the religiosity of the Pueblos and how it informed their architecture:

North House is a communal dwelling. Hence its sacred function is not purely specialized, like the pyramids of Mexico ... in the typical Pueblo way its statement is emphatic and partly concealed ... But its whole is sacred too, and much more than the solid, symmetrical pyramids of Mexico, its syncopated masses clearly dance before the mountain's face. They are active themselves ... the building itself is once again the god of sky and mountain alike, no less wholly embodied in it than at [the ancient Mexican city] at Teotihuacán.[5]

STRATA, too, has spaces that can only be described as sacred. Indoors, a seating area is walled by blocks of Himalayan salt, 9" by 18". Light filters gently through them so beautifully that people think it's some kind of semi-precious stone. The size of the blocks and the fact that they had to be

strata: a desert dwelling

brought all the way from Asia, and sodium being a material regulated by Homeland Security in this size, put logistical skills to work like no other element of the house – beyond that of the bush-hammered silver tiles from Germany or the stone slabs from four different continents. The assemblage of salt blocks is backlit with LEDs. The space takes on a chapel-like ambience, a place of refuge, thought, healing, and silence.

For all its gentle and quiet spaces, steel looms large at STRA-TA, nowhere more so than on the fascia of the cantilevered eaves. True to the bespoke nature of the abode, these were made with great care elsewhere and brought to the site. As this steel weathers it becomes more luminous and beautiful. Two steel centers, located in Ohio and Alabama, played parts in bringing this to reality. The steel was forged in Ohio and put into rolls, then taken to Alabama and cut into the sheets that comprise the cornice today. Construction expert Meek says: "After they cut it, they stretched it just a bit, to help prevent the thin and long steel profiles from moving or contorting over time ... With the assistance of a metallurgically-enhanced batch of steel, we robotically cut the steel with a laser, getting a much cleaner cut." Indeed a look at a photograph of the fascia and you see steel sheets placed at unforgivingly tight tolerances and impeccable evenness, with concealed mechanisms to allow for expansion and contraction of the material in the desert – a place of extreme heat and cold.

Ceilings, bedecked in warm and character-filled Douglas fir, are at different heights in the house depending on whether it is a "public" space or a "private" space – yes, a house this large can have both. A loggia forms the "Main Street" of the house and allows connections to all buildings. A bridge traverses the street to connect the garage with the main house. In both plan and perspective, the house looks very Miesian, if at a much larger residential scale than the German master ever built at.

The clients love water. Outside of the perimeter of the house are a couple of stock ponds. The main interior entry features a gurgling water feature, and of course, there is a pool and spa, whose water surfaces are flush with their surroundings, giving them a surreal feel.

Indoor/outdoor dining is especially appealing in the Desert Southwest owing to its mild, cool nights and relative lack of pesky insects. According to Drewett, Miller and Meek, the ability to eat al fresco was an urgent client demand. Drewett describes one element of this:

Early in the project, the owner showed me this image that stylistically had nothing to do with the project – it was a dining table. Adjacent was an arch that was fairly heavily planted. It felt very "in the landscape," and they wanted a romantic outdoor dining space. They wanted to integrate this into the indoor/outdoor space. As the project unfolded, this particular piece [outdoor trellis] lived in a variety of locations. And then finally we agreed on a location, adjacent to the grill and other appliances ... by the time we designed and constructed this, a lot of the project was completed already. It's a beautiful structural system – cantilevered – with plantings above. It seems to grow out of the site organically.

Despite the bonhomie that exists between the three chief players, there was some constructive cognitive dissonance along the way, as there inevitably is in any collaborative process. Drewett: "I think there were a couple of occasions when we have been a little bit apart on something and one of us would give way. David's like 'You're strong on this, and I trust you.' And yes, vice versa. And I'll say Desert Star came really strong out of the gate. I think we twisted our ankles a little bit with a few missteps initially." For his part, Meek invokes a jingle to describe the process: "As a team, you form, you storm, you norm, you perform!"

Quite a stratum of effort – one that yielded a truly epic residence in the Sonoran Desert.

Notes:
[1] McAra, Catriona, A Surrealist Stratigraphy of Dorothea Tanning's Chasm, Routledge, 2016.
[2] Pauly, Danièle, Le Corbusier: Chapel at Ronchamp, Fondation Le Corbusier, 2020.
[3] Scully, Vincent, American Architecture and Urbanism, Praeger, 1969.
[4] Pratchett, Terry, Jingo, HarperPrism, 1997
[5] Scully, Vincent, Architecture: The Natural and the Manmade, St. Martin's Press, 1991.

interiors

The best word to describe the interiors is associated with a gentlemen's clothier: "Bespoke." STRATA is bespoke in that absolutely everything is custom in its materiality, proportion, and function and made specifically for its occupants. The owners entertain, but they don't live for it. They prefer small gatherings of family and friends and a sense that they have a house big enough to accommodate whatever or whoever comes along.

The design process was an intuitive give-and-take between the designer and architect, with the builder at the ready for testing materials. It was Interior Designer David Michael Miller who was tasked to develop a materials palette relating to the vocabulary established by the architecture. Miller shares:

I vividly recall site visits where we tested different colors of rammed earth blends, various finish types for the mill-scale steel, and several versions of dust on white concrete for floors. These field tests, done with the participation of the owners, design, and construction teams, were essential for testing finishes and colorization. We all understood that getting the core materials properly sorted in the very early days would be essential to the rest of the project's success, as they would become the essential material vocabulary of the house.

Deciding that a narrower palette would produce more impactful buildings and interiors, Drewett and Miller shared preferences for texture and natural materials, providing a firm design foundation. Miller and his team selected limestone, plain sliced white oak, integral color wall plaster, vertical grain fir, and walnut frame millwork. The rich steel qualities in the architecture cued Miller to redouble efforts to bring in additional metals like bronze and hand-hammered brass for a sense of luxury and permanence.

Once the materials palette was established, Miller formulated the interior's identity and character, making broader material design selections for attached interior finishes. Miller and his team designed millwork treatments, developed and illustrated fireplace facades, and created mill panel and door designs for the house. Because of the project's substantial scale and expansive room volumes, Miller focused on making the interiors tactile, welcoming, and luxe. Miller explains:

The broad mix of finishes we selected was intended to bring a sense of richness, calm, and intimacy. The house is very much an architectural statement, and our goal was to soften the room volumes to make the house a warm and tactile place to live.

A series of doors and mill panels Miller's team designed feature specialty wood veneer doors used in prominent locations, including the front entry, multiple barn doors, and interior pivot doors, some with relief pattern details using solid bronze bar stock on the door's surface. Common interior doors and expressed jambs employ wire-brushed vertical grain fir in a horizontal plank design. According to Miller:

The design and materiality of the spaces are carefully conceived early in the design phases, in order to lay in the last curated layers of the interiors – these being rugs, furniture, and art. By investing so much time and energy in selecting materials and designing the interior architectural features of furnished spaces, we created cohesive and well-partnered interiors. The completed interiors provide a feeling of belonging to the building, while still providing subtle surprises and nuances from space to space.

Miller worked with well-respected makers and designers from the U.S. and Western Europe. Miller comments:

We wanted the interior and exterior furnishings to be in a range of styles, not one narrow lane. Although I respect modern furniture classics, and we used some in various parts of the house, I prefer using more bespoke makers like Philip Nimmo, Jean de Merry, and Christian Liaigre, among others.

The designer, who also functioned as a guide with art acquisitions, prioritized scale along with color and content. A color field painting by Paul Jenkins enlivens the main entry space. A large collage piece by Doug and Mike Starn is used in the main dining room, a particularly voluminous space needing a strong piece to anchor it. Other artists include David Kimball Anderson, Charles Arnoldo, Luis Gonzalez Palma, and Mark Klett. Miller acknowledges:

The efforts of everyone on my team, from design assistants to administration and purchasing, were essential in creating and completing this epic commission. I am grateful for each one's contributions. Designer Brian Wieberg, of my team, expertly took my sketches for interiors and millwork and made them into buildable designs. With those drawings in hand, many talented artisans and makers provided beautiful custom pieces for the house, and we relied on their skills and ability to make the project a reality. The fine craft of these makers, along with unique designs authored by our office, conspired to create these truly bespoke interiors.

DMM

interiors

interiors

Interior designer Miller chose a rich assortment of natural materials, including a machined bronze plate, bush-hammered German silver, textured and honed natural stone slab, and various wood species.

A custom sliding teak door opens and closes with silky precision. A cast bronze hand by the artist David Kimball sits on an oxidized steel pedestal. Outside, a grouping of cacti and other desert vegetation lies just beyond.

interiors

In one of the powder rooms, a slab stone sink sits atop a sandblasted elm base cabinet. The wood and stone combine with the rammed earth for a texturally rich palette.

interiors

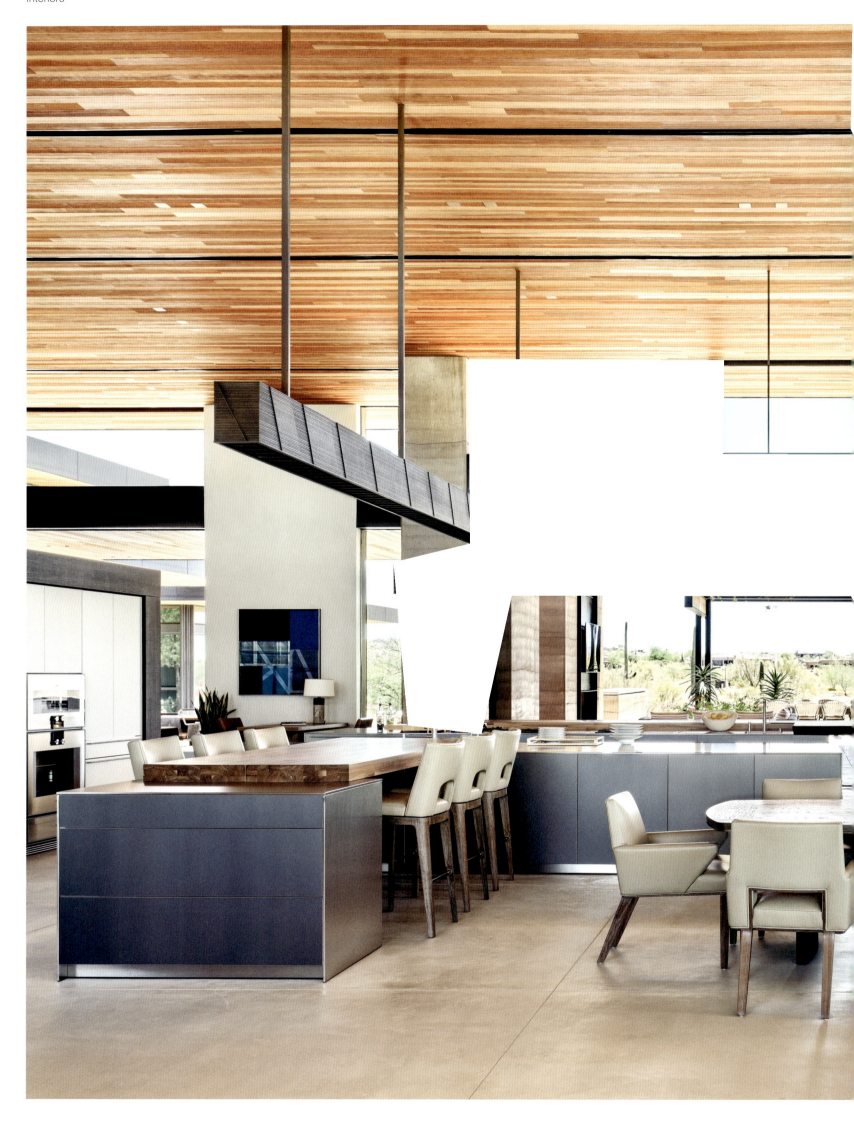

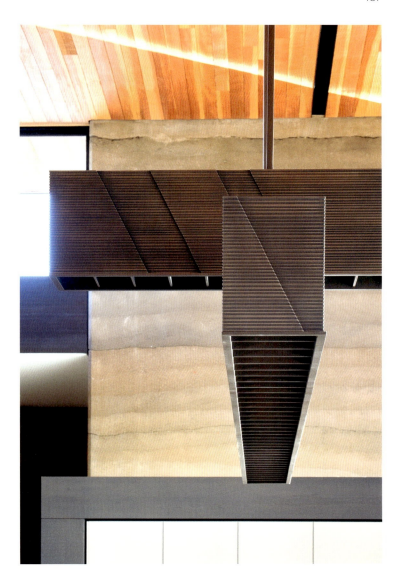

The clients relied on a collaboration with interior designer Miller to furnish the house with an eclectic array of works. A Christian Liaigre desk is adorned with an Alexander Lamont lamp and a painting by Charles Arnoldi.

interiors

The owners took several trips with interior designer Miller to New York, Los Angeles, and local galleries in Phoenix for art acquisition. Cast-resin panels by Arizona artist Mayme Kratz sit on custom bronze and walnut shelves.

interiors

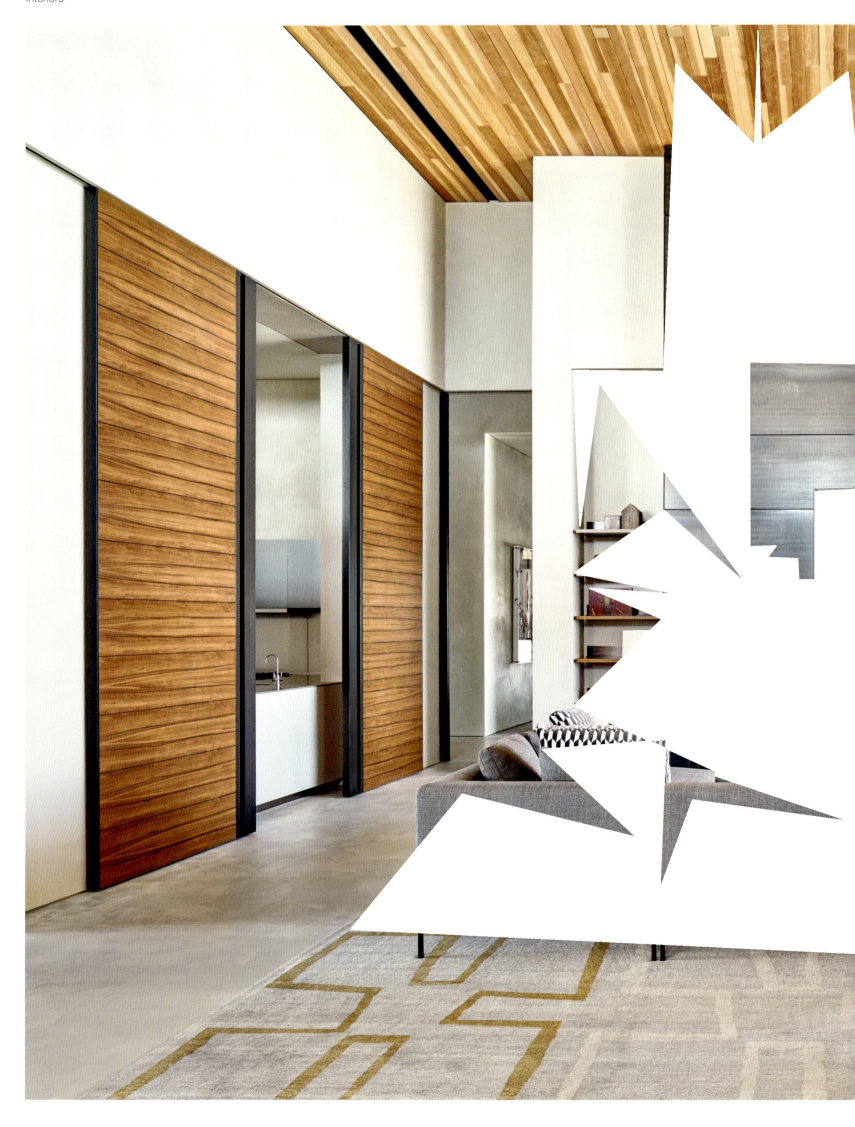

interiors

interiors

interiors

While principally a house for two people, STRATA has extensive guest accommodations for the couple's friends and family. A glimpse into a guest bedroom beyond a planked fir pivot door reveals a photo collage by Marie Navarre. A panel of stacked glass allows additional light in while maintaining privacy.

interiors

A seating area is walled by blocks of Himalayan salt, 9" by 18". Light filters gently through them, giving a chapel-like ambience — a place of refuge, thought, healing, and silence.

interiors

High-polished wall panels and concealed doors allow the office's inner sanctum to be separate from the conference area.

interiors

The office contains several casual seating areas. An accent wall is comprised of raised grain leather with an embedded solid bronze bar stock grid.

interiors

The rammed earth anchoring wall of the primary bedroom is contrasted with lush finishes. Bespoke lamps are by John Wigmore. A rich palette in the room includes printed velvet, woven linen and an all-silk rug by Christopher Farr.

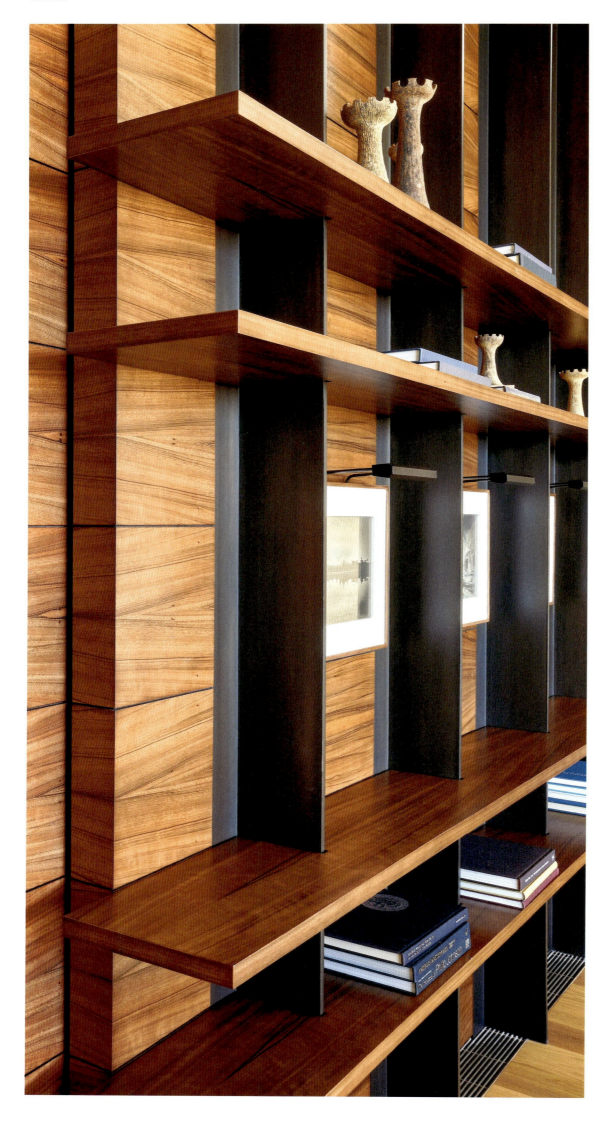

interiors

interiors

interiors

Carved out of a single piece of stone, the bathtub's sculptural form recalls a Jean Arp bird in flight. Black steel-framed bi-fold glass doors allow outdoor access, which is possible given the privacy afforded by 250+ surrounding acres.

interiors

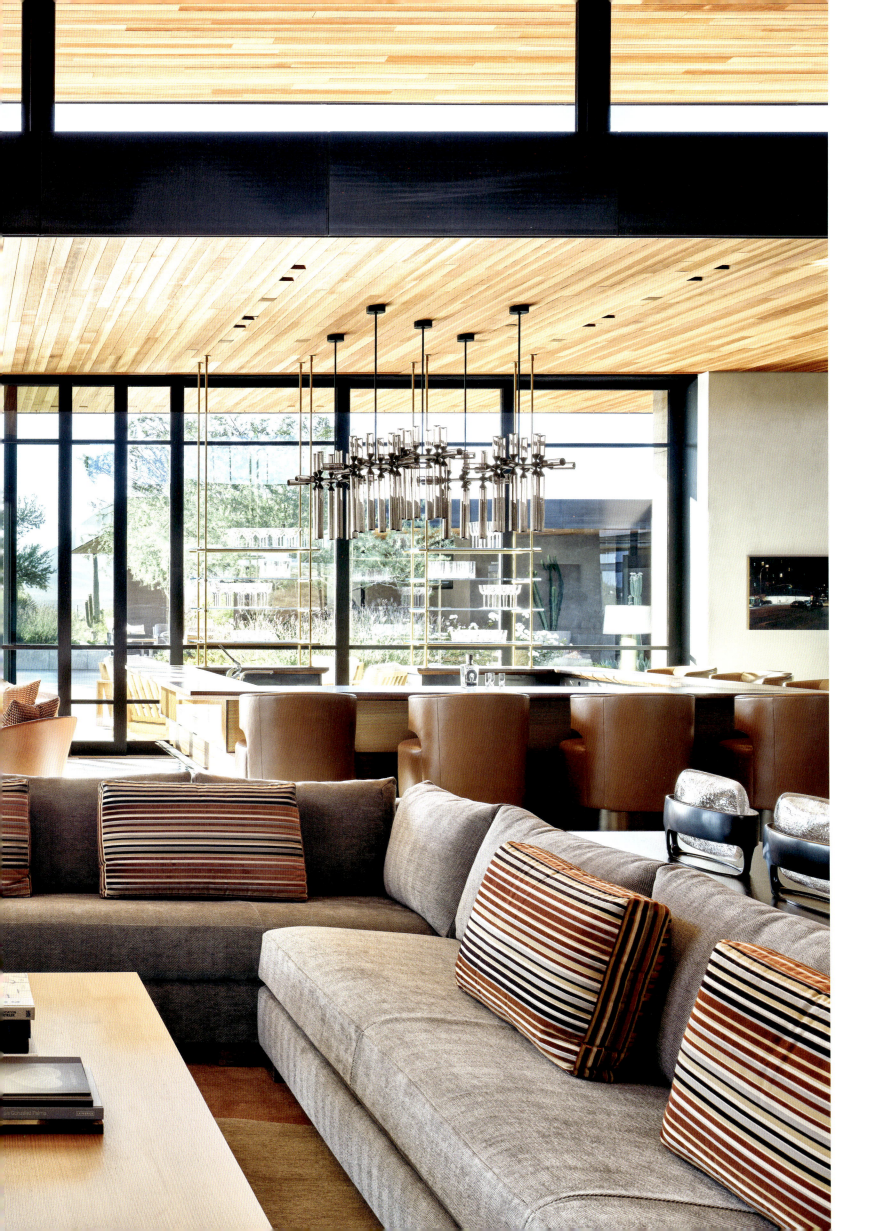

interiors

A sitting area and bar in the main part of the house open to an outdoor lounge and swimming pool. A brass and glass shelving system by Amuneal attaches the bar to the ceiling.

interiors

A bespoke buffet by Philip Nimmo features bush-hammered brass and high-polish walnut veneer. Warm hues in the dining room contrast with a colorful wall collage by Doug and Mike Starn.

interiors

A milled brass inset wall flanked by honed figured stone serves as the dining room focal point. The 17-foot dining table was fashioned from a single piece of walnut by Joseph Jeup.

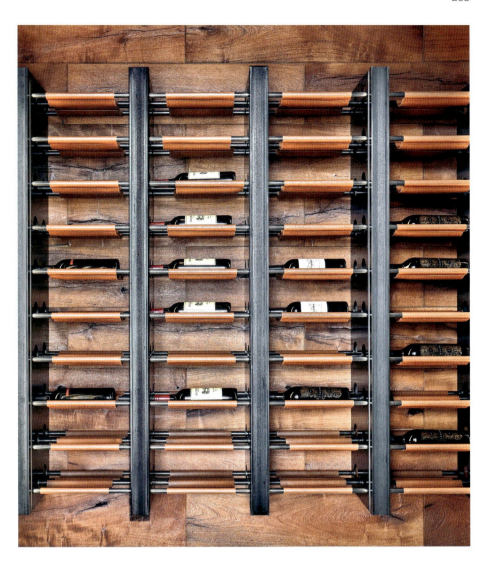

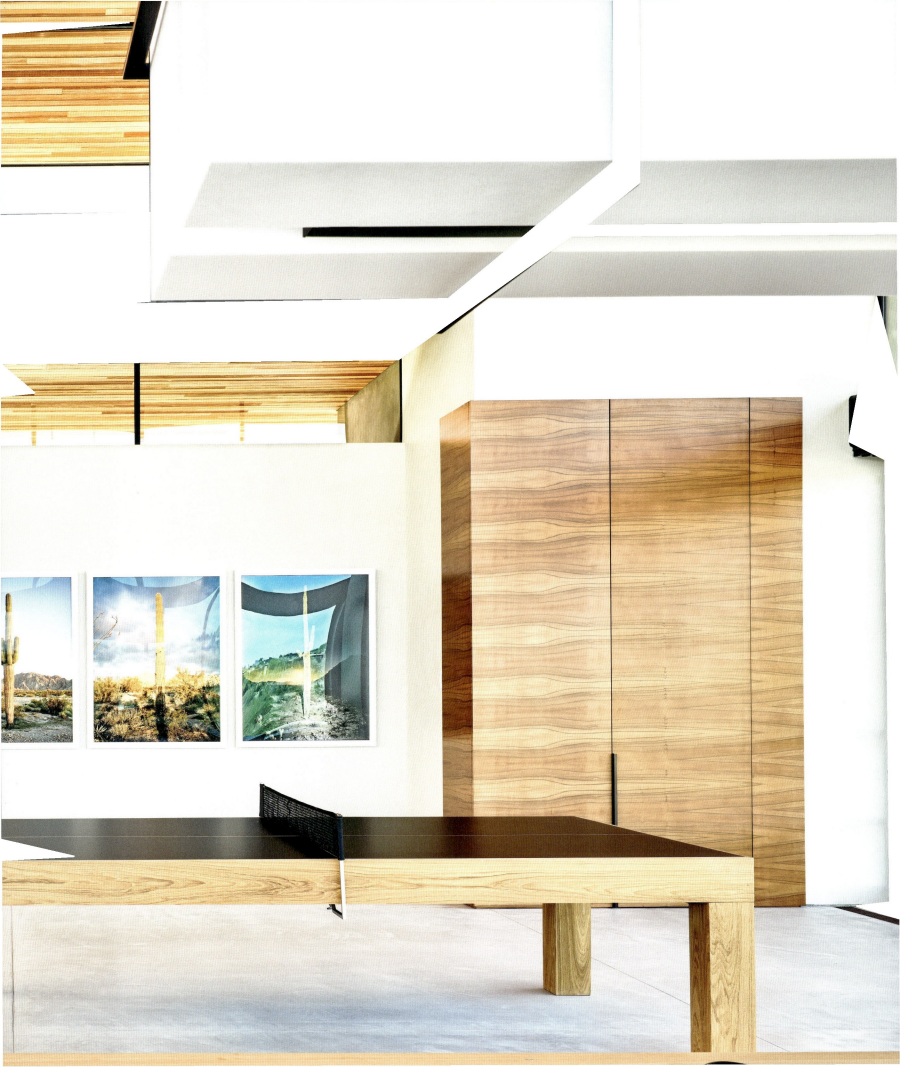

Large, complex, and detail-oriented residences are nothing new to Desert Star Construction. Scale, complexity, and pace proved to be significant challenges of this private residence, demanding uncompromising quality and precision.

A key architectural component strategically and artistically integrated into the design of this house is SIREWALL – a structural insulated rammed earth wall system. Consisting of local soils and cement that have been pneumatically compacted, SIREWALL is earthy in appearance, extremely durable, and helps preserve and protect the residence from the elements. For STRATA, it is a defining element.

Any residence built with rammed earth requires extra attention to detail to ensure that all related building components and systems are coordinated well ahead of time due to the structural permanence of the wall system. Consideration also needs to be given to "future-proofing" to provide the owners flexibility and options in the years and decades ahead. The execution of STRATA required all of this, along with additional layers of complexity in the front-end coordination efforts, specifically the scheduling and programming of the rammed earth walls and protecting them over the project's duration as other construction activities occurred.

STRATA is the epitome of teamwork. DSC led and coordinated with nearly three dozen design, engineering, and specialty disciplines, plus thousands of broader team members working on and off-site, to bring this residence to fruition. The force multipliers that enabled the teams working on this project to complete it quickly and at a high level of quality were a culture of service and humble leadership.

A rare winter storm covers the site and surrounding mountains with snow.

construction

ABOVE Early SIREWALL samples, Jeremy and Jerry Meek **OPPOSITE PAGE TOP** Jeff Berghoff, C.P. Drewett site plan review **OPPOSITE PAGE MIDDLE** Rammed earth discovery trip to Washington, Jerry Meek, and C.P. Drewett **OPPOSITE PAGE BOTTOM** Earthwork for the primary residence building pad

construction

ABOVE AND BELOW Heavy equipment prepares site driveways and building pads **OPPOSITE PAGE TOP** Site preparation includes salvage of native plants

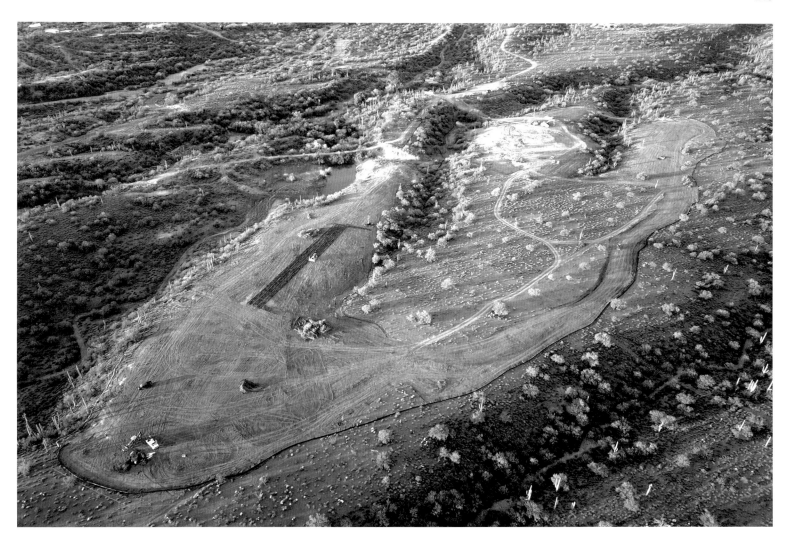

construction

ABOVE A saguaro cactus braced for transport **RIGHT** Saguaros in temporary positions in the salvage nursery **BELOW RIGHT** SIREWALL USA principal Joss Krayenhoff prepares rammed earth material cylinders for strength tests **FURTHER BELOW RIGHT** Rammed earth material moves via hopper into mock-up wall forms **BOTTOM RIGHT** Deliberating rammed earth wall color schemes against the backdrop of the mountains, David Miller and C.P. Drewett

construction

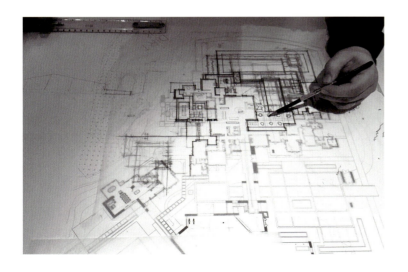

ABOVE A friendly flamingo takes a dip in the proposed pool location
LEFT Preliminary floor plans are sketched by architect C.P. Drewett
OPPOSITE PAGE STRATA preliminary floor plan is chalked on-site

construction

A portion of the construction schedule in Gantt Chart format details over 2,000 activities

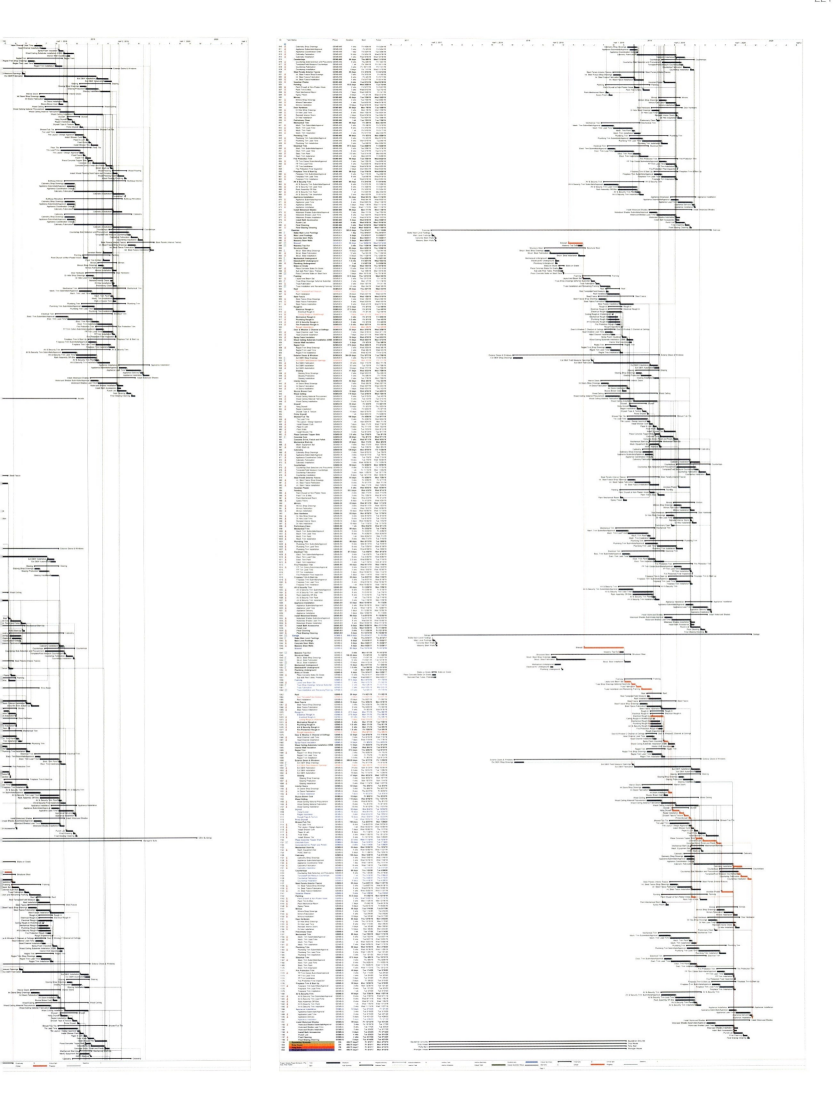

construction

OPPOSITE PAGE TOP Chalk lines reveal future walls; a telehandler suspends a mock-up steel fascia panel **OPPOSITE PAGE BOTTOM** A paper submission is prepared for municipal approval for one of the primary buildings **RIGHT** Horizon views are confirmed through proposed door openings at the primary living area **MIDDLE** A pool and primary water feature are tarped and filled with water **BOTTOM** PVC frames help visualize future view corridors

construction

ABOVE Rammed earth wall formwork
LEFT Workers inside the rammed earth forms prepare for compaction
OPPOSITE PAGE TOP Rammed earth material is mixed and delivered to the telebelt **OPPOSITE PAGE BOTOM** A completed rammed earth wall, formwork partially removed, reveals a compound chamfered header

construction

ABOVE Workers prepare rebar for the foundation of retaining walls
BELOW Specialty concrete is placed via boom pump in the linear reflecting pool adjacent to the dining gallery
OPPOSITE PAGE A telebelt extends through the arcade preparing for material

FOLLOWING SPREAD Concrete slurry placed via boom pump will encase ductwork to minimize future differential settlement

construction

construction

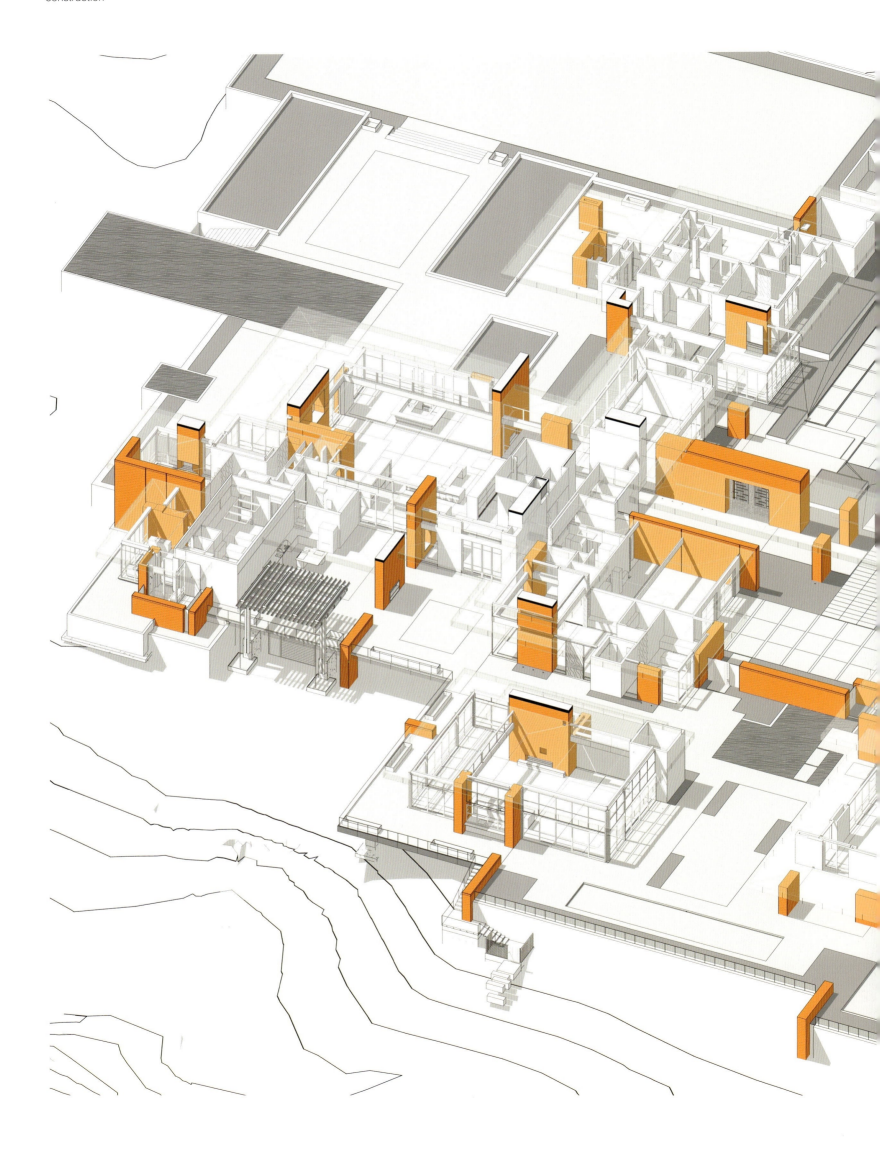

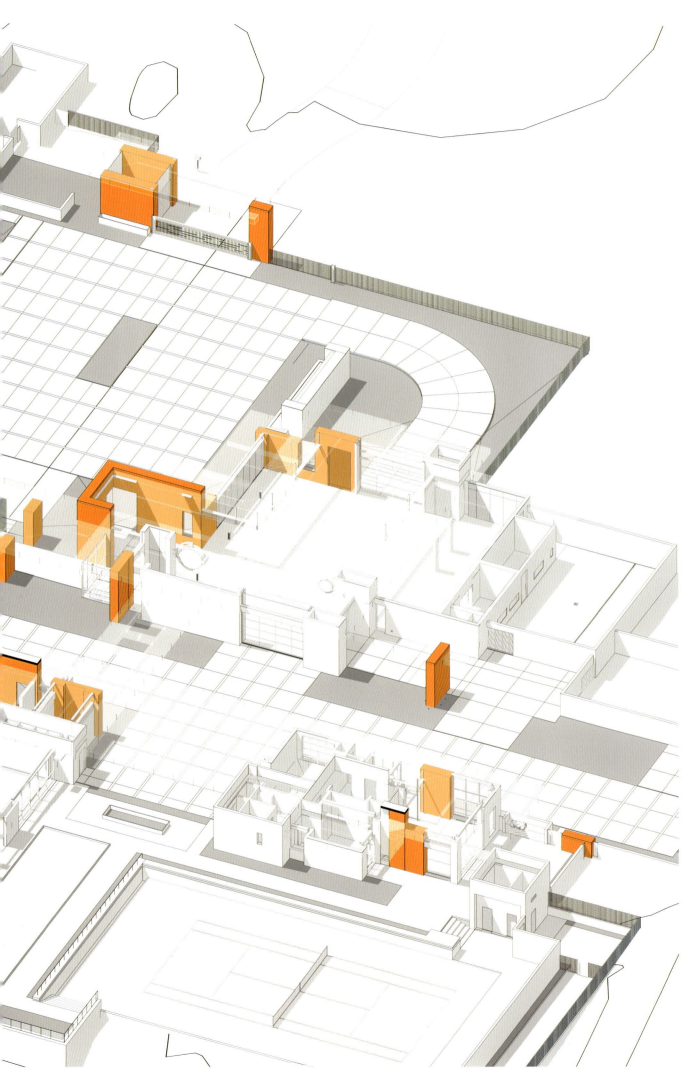

The project's rammed earth walls are highlighted in orange

FOLLOWING SPREAD Wood trusses are set in place integrating with the structural steel, glulam beams, and rammed earth walls

construction

construction

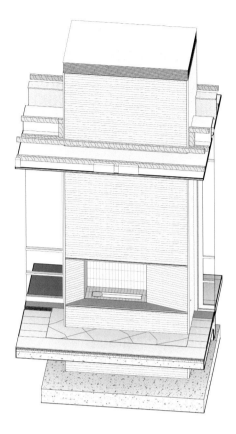

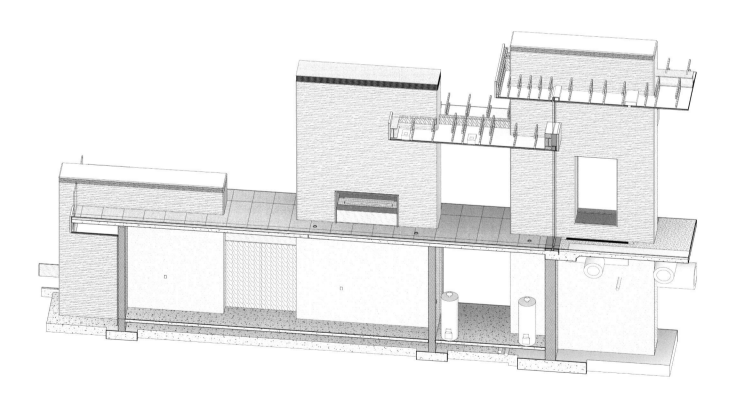

SIREWALL coordination drawings from the architectural set

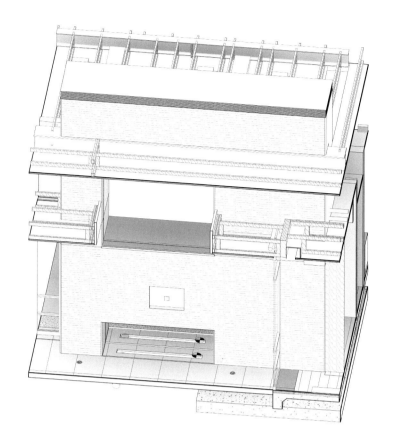

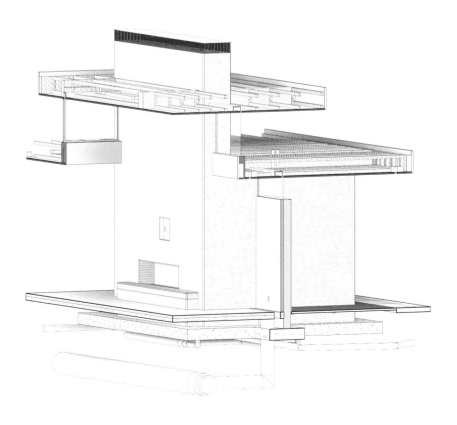

construction

construction

PREVIOUS SPREAD Structural steel is set in place via crane on high rooflines
LEFT A cantilevered structural steel beam, integral to the ramming process, protrudes from rammed earth wall formwork
ABOVE A site visit by a desert native

construction

ABOVE LEFT A rammed earth mock-up, Jeremy and Jerry Meek **ABOVE RIGHT** David Miller and C.P. Drewett review a full-scale mock-up of wine room racking and lighting assembly

BELOW LEFT Custom wood samples are reviewed on-site by the design team **BELOW RIGHT** Rolls and sheets of architectural steel before laser cutting and fabrication

ABOVE Brian Wieberg and David Miller review a wine rack mock-up
BELOW LEFT Metallurgically optimized steel ensures clean cuts with robotic lasers **BELOW RIGHT** A custom-fabricated boom safely sets steel fascia panels onto adjustable mounting brackets below

construction

LEFT The building exoskeleton reveals precise 4-inch grid alignment of speakers, subwoofers, lighting, fire sprinklers, and other elements
RIGHT Workers on a scissor lift prepare to place steel windows into a rough opening

construction

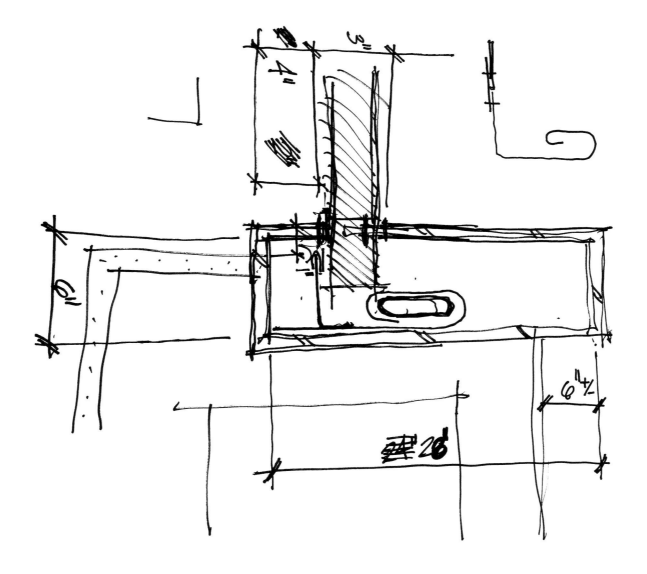

OPPOSITE PAGE TOP Fabricated structural steel members are staged at the site **TOP RIGHT** Team DSC superintendent Matt Mehall stands near the install of a pedestal deck system **MIDDLE** A boom pump delivers concrete for the tennis court's post-tensioned, monolithic concrete slab **BOTTOM LEFT** The design and construction teams review finished wood ceiling planks **BOTTOM RIGHT** Protection is in place in the arcade for the finishing touches applied to the wet concrete **SKETCH** A sketch of a concealed track jamb detail for the garage

construction

construction

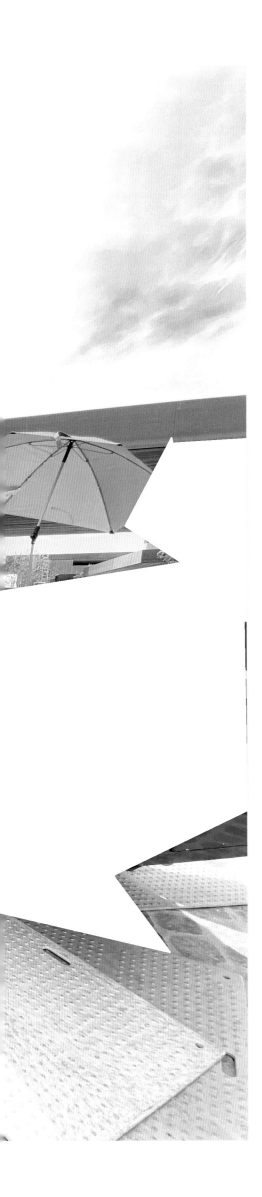

PREVIOUS SPREAD *A trade contractor appreciation lunch hosted by Team DSC at the site of the future tennis court*

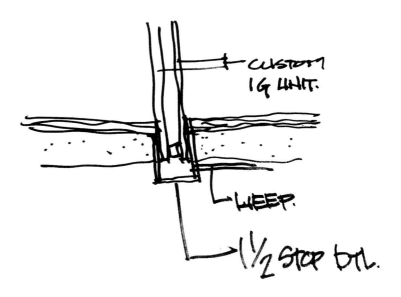

LEFT *A spider crane outfitted with a high-powered suction cup places a large-format piece of glass*
ABOVE *Large-format, custom glass windows are positioned on site ahead of installation with an array of powered suction cups*
SKETCH *Architectural sketch for varying channel-set glazing conditions and terminations*
BELOW *Steel window frames are installed and ready for glass*

construction

construction

PREVIOUS SPREAD A cantilevered structural steel trellis with integral lighting, planters, and irrigation is set in place

ABOVE LEFT C.P. Drewett and Drewett Works team members Melissa Wastell and Alyssa Rowley approach the site **ABOVE RIGHT** DSC Project Manager Josh Gleason finalizes on-site work ahead of the owners' move-in day **BELOW LEFT** Jerry Meek and DSC Superintendent Matt Mehall on-site at the outdoor entertaining deck

BELOW RIGHT DSC Superintendents Jared Bazzell and Matt Mehall on-site during initial foundation work **RIGHT PAGE** Christmas festivities at STRATA gathered three generations of builders: Jeremy Meek (left) and Jon Meek (right) flank Team DSC co-founders Jerry Meek (middle) and Gerald Meek (seated)

photography credits

Steel, bronze, and rammed earth form a layered vignette repeated throughout the house.

The entry is a study in textures and contrasts.

Glass walls open the great room's bar and lounge to mountain views.

A bocce court is tucked between the arcade and wellness center.

Multiple rooflines converge at the garage.

Perched above the desert, the residence emulates the desert landscape.

The front entry is flanked by a guest wing (right) and a loggia leading to the garage (left).

A serene water feature flanks the wellness center entry.

Mass, void, and the architecture's horizontal nature express a close relationship to the desert floor and the mountains beyond.

A welcoming entry presents a simple materials palette – rammed earth, Douglas fir, and limestone.

The entry takes on the hues of the desert sun.

Owners view of the entry features the primary materials palette – steel, wood, concrete, and rammed earth.

A cross breeze while dining is provided by a 52-foot-long teak pocket door and sliding glass panels on the opposing side.

Furniture-like floating millwork creates a spacious ambiance.

Bulthaup millwork and custom linear light fixtures define the chef's kitchen.

A cozy keeping room sits adjacent to the kitchen.

A fully bespoke glazing system in the great room becomes part of the overall architecture.

Bi-fold glass doors in the primary bathroom open to the arid desert breeze.

Operable glass doors in the primary bathroom transition to stone before touching rammed earth.

A sliding glass door pockets between the TV and rammed earth wall.

photography credits

French casement windows allow light and breezes into the guest living room.

Pocketing glass walls open to meld an indoor bar and lounge with the outdoor living space.

A marriage of contained plantings and architectural massing.

Overhangs protect living spaces from the summer sun.

A cantilever shades a guest suite patio.

A view of the lap pool looking toward the mountains.

Integration of steel to rammed earth at the great room fireplace.

A Lautner knife-edge pool situated outside the office.

Outdoor entertaining areas meld seamlessly into indoor living spaces.

A cantilevered trellis and raised planters define outdoor dining.

A dining trellis and rammed-earth fireplace wall.

Outdoor living spaces lead to the adjacent arcade building.

The arrival drive leads to a garage (left) and wellness center (right).

A rammed earth enclosure displays one of the owners' favorite cars.

Clerestory glass and a floating roof bring light into the garage.

An upper roof floats above the car display, situated under a lower ceiling.

An expansive entry court features individual desert gardens carved from the space.

Situated at the edge of a natural wash, the residence appears to levitate.

The arcade transforms into an open-air pavilion.

Strategic exterior lighting showcases the arcade's structure.

Floating limestone highlights the view corridor between his office and the arcade.

A passageway between buildings features garden-like desert plantings

Cantilevered roof forms hover above glass and rammed earth walls.

Custom steel gates beckon visitors to enter.

Desert views become art for the lush entertaining space

Layers of compacted earth are visible in the rammed earth walls.

An impactful entry introduces the house to guests.

A hand-hammered brass overlay credenza by Normandie Woodworks; painting by Paul Jenkins.

A cast bronze hand by artist David Kimball sits on an oxidized steel pedestal.

A double-sided fireplace wall and floating wall panel with media monitor embrace an elegant sitting area.

A slab stone sink sits atop a sandblasted elm base cabinet.

A chef-style Bulthaup kitchen provides space for multiple cooks and offers various dining places.

Custom linear pendant lights moderate the voluminous kitchen.

The machined bronze custom light fixtures feature louver blades.

Ribbed glass directs and diffuses light.

A Christian Liaigre desk is adorned by an Alexander Lamont lamp and painting by Charles Arnoldi.

A cozy keeping room with modern furnishings allows the owners to relax in a more intimate volume of space.

Cast-resin panels by Arizona artist Mayme Kratz sit on custom bronze and walnut shelves.

A mill-scale steel-clad fireplace dominates the keeping room; behind bespoke walnut barn doors (left) is a secondary kitchen.

The bespoke nature of common interior doors can be seen in this detail; hardware by Chant Hardware.

photography credits

A blind door to a concealed bar was designed in vertical grain Douglas fir to complement other interior doors.

The powder room is anchored by a floating vanity structure built in leathered quartzite.

The guest living room offers views of the entry courtyard.

A wall art series by Louis Gonzales Palma and a cast resin panel by Mayme Kratz highlight the guest living room.

Polished onyx and backlit glass provide a smartly lit vanity treatment in the powder room.

A glimpse into a guest bedroom beyond a planked fir pivot door reveals a photo collage by Marie Navarre.

Dust on white concrete, integral color wall plaster, and a rammed earth fireplace create a tranquil guest suite.

A cantilevered walnut base cabinet and a leathered stone top highlight a guest bath.

Vanity cabinets in secondary baths float 12" above the dust on white concrete floor.

Guest room furnishings are simple and practical; painting (left) is by Mark Pomilio and resin panel (right) is by Chris Richter.

A rammed earth fireplace wall with steel fascia is the focal point of the wellness lounge.

Simple reclined seating is nestled by the fireplace; woven copper floor light by Alexander Lamont.

A series of white oak doors subdivide individually functioning spaces in the wellness lounge; resin wall art by Hunt Retigg.

Himalayan salt blocks bring healing properties to the spa-like salt room in the wellness center.

Furnished in modern pieces, the conference lounge has a patio view; painting by Mala Breuer.

Modern styling defines the conference room; the console is high-polished wood veneer and bronze.

A polished cast-bronze lamp by Cast Design serves as a modern accent.

High-polished wall panels and concealed doors allow the office's inner sanctum to be separate from the conference area.

The office lounge is outfitted with designer chairs clustered around a polished agate and bronze cocktail table.

Storage in the light-filled office is behind high-polished cabinetry.

A dark wall comprises raised grain leather with an embedded solid bronze bar stock grid.

The anchoring wall of the primary bedroom is rammed earth and contrasts with lush finishes; bespoke lamps by John Wigmore.

A rich palette in the owners' suite includes printed velvet, woven linen, and an all-silk rug by Christopher Farr.

An intricate millwork wall of walnut and oxidized bronze is the highlight of the owners' bedroom.

The wall unit forms a partition between the bedroom, adjoining bathroom, and closet.

Three daguerreotypes by Binh Danh with integrated lighting are featured in the display shelves.

A modern interpretation of a western whipstitch pattern is embedded into several feature doors.

The owners' closet comprises custom millwork and an Italian closet system by Rimadesio; walnut baffles suspend pendant lights by Alison Berger.

Several display storage components organize the main closet.

A custom walnut veneer and bronze dressing mirror are backlit with resin lighting.

Rammed earth walls flank the owners' bathing area; the tub, carved from a single block of stone, is a functional objet d'art.

Tiles beyond the tub are a bush-hammered German silver.

Vanities are supported by structural piers that run from floor to ceiling supplying power and concealing plumbing.

Walnut-veneer vanities feel minimal and untethered.

Her office, adjacent to the owners' suite, features a painting by Carrie Marill.

The leather-wrapped credenza is from BDDW.

Her office opens to a patio with teak swivel chairs by David Sutherland.

The entertainment zone glass walls retract into the building for an indoor-outdoor experience.

A sitting area and bar in the main house open to an outdoor lounge and swimming pool.

A brass and glass shelving system by Amuneal joins the bar to the ceiling.

photography credits

The custom bar incorporates a walnut top, an apron of backlit laminated glass, and a bronze foot.

A bespoke buffet by Philip Nimmo features bush-hammered brass and high-polish walnut veneer.

Warm hues in the dining room add an inviting ambiance; wall collage by Doug and Mike Starn.

A milled bronze inset wall flanked with honed figured stone serves as the dining room focal point.

The 17-foot dining table was fashioned from a single piece of walnut by Joseph Jeup.

The leathered quartzite arcade bar has an illuminated glass panel inset in front; bar chairs by Craig Bassam.

Native mesquite wood wall paneling, mill-scale steel, and hand-sewn leather cradles store the owners' wine collection; vertical supports are integrally lit.

A custom shuffleboard and poker table add to the recreation options in the arcade.

The arcade includes teak game tables by James Perse; desert photos by Mark Klett.

A desert wash flanks the perimeter of the desert dwelling.

Werner Segarra
PHOTOGRAPHER

Werner Segarra, of Puerto Rican and German descent, completed his formal studies in photography at the Art Institute of Philadelphia in 1995. During his youth, he lived throughout Europe and Saudi Arabia, an experience that provided him with a multicultural sensibility that can be appreciated in his work.

The photographer moved back to Puerto Rico, where he started working as a full-time commercial photographer and rediscovered his roots. Segarra currently lives in Phoenix, Arizona, and has a successful career with an extensive roster of high-profile clients. He also has a second home in the remote town of Huasabas, Mexico, a location that provided him with the inspiration for his Art Photography exhibition "Vaqueros de la Cruz del Diablo." His keen eye for detail and composition, his mastery of light and technique, and his superb taste and respect for cultural idiosyncrasies have helped him develop a unique visual vocabulary. His latest work, "Mi Herencia" (Puerto Rico), celebrates the richness of the island's coffee industry tradition, family values, mourning, and religion.

project credits

BUILDING
Name: STRATA

LOCATION
Phoenix, Arizona, USA

DATES
Design: 2015-2017
Completion: 2020

AREA
Lot size: > 250 acres
Building size: > 70,000 sq. ft.

DESIGNERS
Architecture:
Drewett Works
Design Team:
C.P. Drewett
Melissa Wastell
Rob Banach
Interior Design:
David Michael Miller Associates
Design Team:
David Michael Miller
Brian Wieberg
Shelley Behrhorst

CONSTRUCTION
Builder: Desert Star Construction
Construction Team:
Carol Meek
Devin Moon
Jared Bazzell
Jeremy Meek
Jerry Meek
Josh Gleason
Kieran Davern
Louie Sanchez
Matt Glover
Matt Mehall
Matt Rulapaugh
Mike Rulapaugh

CONSULTANTS
Landscape Designer:
Berghoff Design Group
Erin Leslie
Jeff Berghoff
Nancie Vollmer
Lighting Designer:
Creative Designs In Lighting
Brendon Smith
Mark Mueller
Walter Spitz
Structural Engineer:
PH Structural
Dominic Petrocelli
Marcus Hayward
Civil Engineer:
Wood, Patel & Associates
Nicholas Brown
Mechanical Engineer:
Peterson Consulting Engineers
Plumbing Engineer: Peterson Consulting Engineers
Electrical Engineer: Peterson Consulting Engineers

TRADE CONTRACTOR & VENDOR HONOR ROLL
A.J. Decker Construction
Accent Design & Manufacturing
Allaire
Art Solutions & Installations
AZ Custom Glass
Bulthaup Scottsdale
Clyde Hardware
Cook & Solis Construction
Cyber Technology Group
Encore Steel
Golka Electric
Hope's Windows
Hopper Finishes
Jake's Custom Framing
James Loudspeaker
Kip Merritt Designs
Larson Solutions
Levake Concrete
Linear Fine Woodworking
Native Resources International
Phoenician Pools
Premiere Wood Floors
Quail Plumbing
Saguaro Drywall
Simonson Painting
SIREWALL USA
Stockett Tile and Granite
Sutter Masonry
Tom Nichols Excavating

BOOK PRODUCTION TEAM
Elizabeth Drewett
Langdon Drewett
Lily Motes
Nancy Erdmann

company profiles

Drewett Works is about an architecture of time and place. An award-winning Arizona-based firm specializing in high-end residential and hospitality projects, Drewett Works unlocks the mysteries of the site to yield buildings that express the deepest essences of the client, the venue, and the intended uses. A large portion of the firm's body of work is in the Sonoran Desert of Arizona, a natural cornucopia that is a dream canvas for any architect. Founder and lead architect C.P. Drewett brings to the table a passion rooted in his childhood, working with his Marine Corps aviator father, also a woodworking hobbyist, to create objects of lasting beauty. His family moved 18 times during his childhood, giving him a deep sense of respect for regional architectural traditions while fostering excitement about making an impact on a local scale. The 21-person Drewett studio is diverse and brings a keen variety of perspectives and experiences to the design process. The firm's design approach is restrained and reductive – Drewett edits down the massing and materials palettes to get at the core of the expressive idea. Inspired by the grandees of modernist design without being beholden to them, Drewett Works creates houses that will grace the landscape long after the initial clients and designers are gone. It is design for the ages.

David Michael Miller Associates is interior design characterized by a fusion with the building's architectural context. This stance has meant David Michael Miller has an exceptional history of collaborating with architects, none more so than with C.P. Drewett. Led by David, the studio strives to create interiors that are rich, unique, understated and reflective of the client's essences. David's consistent avoidance of design trend extremes, and his desire to maximize the greatest potential of each new project, make his work a timeless distillation of style. For David, the ideal ingredients of authentic and relevant interior design can be characterized by a relationship to geographic and cultural influences, as well as the client's own lifestyle and color sensibilities. A careful blend of these elements provides for an original, personal and thoughtful design aesthetic. Ultimately, it is this designed environment in which the client will live, and for that reason, the interiors should reflect the client's own identity and passions.

For **Desert Star Construction**, every project is an independent undertaking. Utilizing the systems and processes developed and honed since its founding 45 years ago, Team DSC® has a deep affinity for collaborating with design teams to realize its clients' vision. Decades of experience have led the firm to understand the subtle ins and outs of luxury custom home building, and its vast network of craftspeople and vendors allows it to create authentic abodes honoring each designer's and owner's intent, be they in traditional Southwestern architectural styles or the modernist architecture described in this book.

A family-founded and operated firm with deep roots in Arizona, Team DSC leads a coterie of craftspeople who work through the inevitable challenges that present themselves on any one-of-a-kind project. Under the trademarked moniker The DSC Standard®, the firm's construction professionals proactively anticipate and seek out problems to enable swift progress on the fine custom homes and Personal Resorts® that it is commissioned to construct. Team DSC's track record of integrity and experience working with the nation's leading designers speaks for itself – it is the "go-to" bespoke construction company, a business whose passion for the built environment, excellence in execution, and stewardship on behalf of its clients is evidenced in every project it undertakes.

contributors

C.P. Drewett, AIA, NCARB
DREWETT WORKS PRESIDENT AND FOUNDING ARCHITECT

Driven by a passion for design, mathematics, and physics, architect C.P. Drewett, AIA, NCARB, has established himself as one of the most sought-after professionals in his field. Pushing the edge of everything he does, he is known for his innovative, compelling work and modernist style. In 2001, C.P. launched his award-winning architectural firm, Drewett Works, in Scottsdale, Arizona, and has amassed a vast portfolio that focuses on the upper end of residential, commercial, and masterplan projects. C.P.'s deep respect for regional architectural traditions and his reputation for creating artful, timeless, and innovative designs have earned him respect among his peers and discerning clientele.

David Michael Miller
PROFESSIONAL MEMBER, ASID
FOUNDER AND PRINCIPAL OF DAVID MICHAEL MILLER ASSOCIATES

David Michael Miller is founder and principal of David Michael Miller Associates, a residential interior design firm located in Scottsdale, Arizona. The firm, created in 1989, has an established reputation for drawing on the natural surrounding environment to inform the interior design. David was born and raised in the Middle Western United States, and received his design training in Chicago, Illinois at Ray College. Inspired by the American architect Frank Lloyd Wright, David's education in interior design coincided with his study of this maverick native architect. It is likely due to the influence of this architect that David's work is consistently respectful of, and integrated to, the architectural settings in which his interiors exist. David's restrained aesthetic sensibilities, and his adherence to the use of natural materials, help to create interiors that are understated, unpretentious and stylistically enduring.

Jerry Meek
FOUNDER & CEO OF DESERT STAR CONSTRUCTION

Jerry Meek is the founder and CEO of Desert Star Construction, established in 1978. He is known by clients and industry colleagues as having "the best team in the luxury home business." The last decade has been focused on continuous growth and expansion of the DSC brand, whose results have been published in more than 30 magazines and earned honors such as multiple Gold Nugget Awards, Phoenix Home & Garden Home of the Year, Southwest Contractor, and NAHB Custom Home of the Year. In 2017, Jerry was the first-ever luxury custom home builder to receive Phoenix Home & Garden's Masters of the Southwest, an award program in its 30th year that recognizes the best in design and craftsmanship. Jerry also leads Desert Star Concierge, a proactive maintenance and service business for completed homes and Personal Resorts®. Jerry also served as the founding president of the Phoenix Dream Center Foundation, which aids young survivors of human trafficking. Today, he continues to enjoy time with Carol, his wife of over 42 years, in Cave Creek, Arizona, and has two adult sons.

Jeremy Meek
PRESIDENT OF DESERT STAR CONSTRUCTION

Jeremy Meek literally grew up with Desert Star Construction in his DNA and is currently serving Team DSC® as president. Since starting work at nine years old at one dollar per hour, Jeremy has worked alongside Team DSC to advance the company's long-standing commitment to providing clients with trademark DSC excellence – The DSC Standard® – in the most technically complex and finely appointed luxury homes in Arizona. In addition to a bachelor's degree in Construction Management from Arizona State University and a Master of Philosophy in Engineering for Sustainable Development from the University of Cambridge in England, Jeremy has completed Stanford University's Advanced Project Management program, the premier certification for program and project management in the 21st-century context. Jeremy was the first LEED for Homes Accredited Professional registered in Arizona.

James Moore McCown

James Moore McCown is a Boston-based architectural journalist who writes for numerous design publications including *Metropolis, Architect's Newspaper* and *Architectural Digest AD PRO*. He has collaborated with Oscar Riera Ojeda on several books including the Architecture in Detail series which comprised two volumes: *Colors* and *Spaces*. McCown studied journalism at Loyola University New Orleans and holds an ALM (Master's Degree) in the history of art and architecture from Harvard University, where his thesis on modern Brazilian architecture received an Honorable Mention, Dean's Award, Best ALM Thesis (2007).

In addition to being a journalist, McCown consults with architecture firms on marketing, publicity and thought leadership programs. A native of Mobile, Alabama, he lives in Newton, Massachusetts.

Oscar Riera Ojeda

Oscar Riera Ojeda is an editor and designer based in the US, China, and Argentina. Born in 1966, in Buenos Aires, he moved to the United States in 1990. Since then he has published over three hundred books, assembling a remarkable body of work notable for its thoroughness of content, timeless character, and sophisticated and innovative craftsmanship. Oscar Riera Ojeda's books have been published by many prestigious publishing houses across the world, including Birkhäuser, Byggförlaget, The Monacelli Press, Gustavo Gili, Thames & Hudson, Rizzoli, Damiani, Page One, ORO editions, Whitney Library of Design, and Taschen. He is also the creator of numerous architectural book series, including Ten Houses, Contemporary World Architects, The New American House and The New American Apartment, Architecture in Detail, and Single Building. His work has received many international awards, in-depth reviews, and citations. He is a regular contributor and consultant for several publications in the field. In 2001 Oscar Riera Ojeda founded ORO Editions company for which he was responsible of the completion of nearly one hundred titles. In 2008 he established his current publishing venture, Oscar Riera Ojeda Publishers, a firm with fifteen employees and locations across three continents.

book credits

Graphic Design by Florencia Damilano
Art Direction by Oscar Riera Ojeda
Copy Editing by Kit Maude and Michael W. Phillips Jr.

Know more
about STRATA:

OSCAR RIERA OJEDA
PUBLISHERS

Team DSC®, Personal Resorts®, The DSC Standard®, Building the Best Better®, and Builder for Life® are registered service marks of Desert Star Construction, Inc. The Author has used these service marks within this book with permission from Desert Star Construction, Inc. SIREWALL® is a registered trademark of Sirewall, Inc. The Author has used this trademark within this book with permission from Sirewall, Inc.

Copyright © 2023 by Oscar Riera Ojeda Publishers Limited
ISBN 978-1-946226-69-3
Published by Oscar Riera Ojeda Publishers Limited
Printed in China

Oscar Riera Ojeda Publishers Limited
Unit 1331, Beverley Commercial Centre,
87-105 Chatham Road South, Tsim Sha Tsui, Kowloon, Hong Kong

Production Offices
Suit 19, Shenyun Road,
Nanshan District, Shenzhen 518055, China

International Customer Service & Editorial Questions: +1-484-502-5400

www.oropublishers.com | www.oscarrieraojeda.com
oscar@oscarrieraojeda.com

All rights reserved. No part of this book may be reproduced, stored in a retrieval system, or transmitted in any form or by any means, including electronic, mechanical, photocopying or microfilming, recording, or otherwise (except that copying permitted by Sections 107 and 108 of the U.S. Copyright Law and except by reviewers for the public press) without written permission from the publisher.